And the Journey Begins

And the Journey Begins

Cyril Axelrod

Douglas
McLean

Published by

DOUGLAS McLEAN

8 St John Street, Coleford, Gloucestershire GL16 8AR

© Cyril Axelrod 2005

Set in 12.5/16pt Monotype Garamond

Typeset by Red Lizard Ltd., Redditch, Worcestershire

Printed in England by
The Cromwell Press Ltd., Trowbridge, Wiltshire

British Library Cataloguing in Publication Data

A CIP catalogue record for this book is available from the British Library

Trade Paperback: ISBN 0-946252-55-6

Hardcover: ISBN 0-946252-58-0

With grateful acknowledgements to the following for permission to reprint the material listed:

Faber and Faber Limited for lines from 'The Rock' by T. S. Eliot © T. S. Eliot 1934
The Peterborough Evening Telegraph for the picture 'Blessing the Turf'
John Weaver for photographs taken at St John the Evangelist Church, Islington, London, 2004
Deaf Community of Cape Town for photographs taken there in 2004
Roman Catholic Diocese of Westminster Deaf Service, London, for photographs taken at Westminster Cathedral on 27 November 2004

Every effort has been made to trace copyright holders and to obtain their permission for the use of copyright material. The author and publisher apologise for any errors or omissions in the above list and would be grateful if notified of any corrections that should be incorporated in future reprints or editions of this book.

Dedication

For Dawn Raphaely and Claire Baecher, and in memory of
my beloved mother and father, Yetta and Abe Axelrod.

Acknowledgements

The creation of my autobiography would not have been possible without the help and support of my lifelong friend Dr Robert Simmons. I express my heartfelt gratitude to him for his great patience and for giving so much time to work with me on my book.

I also thank Jack Gannon for the guidance he gave me and Rev. Larry Kaufmann who was the first to know of my oncoming blindness and who has remained a constant friend. I am particularly grateful for his firm encouragement throughout and for reading and checking my manuscripts.

My thanks go to Rev. Philip Dabney and Rev. Jim Wallace and all at the Redemptorist Holy Redeemer College, Washington DC for allowing me to use the library computer to begin writing this biography in 1996.

My dear cousins Dawn Raphaely and Claire Baecher have given their encouragement and spurred me on with their belief that my story should be told. So have many others, far too numerous to name here. I thank them all.

My most sincere thanks go to Deafblind UK for their generous Millenium Award that provided my computer and other equipment that has made it possible for me to complete my autobiography. My thanks also go to Mrs Jackie Hicks for the support she and her staff have given me during the critical time of my becoming totally blind.

I am especially grateful to my editor, Lyn Atkinson, whose insight and understanding of deafblindness has been so important to me during the creation of this book. I also thank her husband and my publisher Doug McLean who gave most valuable guidance and support in taking it into print. I thank them both for their friendship and warm hospitality on my frequent visits to their home for 'editorial' meetings. I am also deeply grateful to Liz Hansford for her skilled help and interpreting during these meetings.

Thanks also go to William Richards, Yvonne Shorthouse and Mike Darton for their editing and proof reading assistance at different stages of the book's development, and to Miriam Barnett for her helpful guidance.

All my confrères, and members of my Redemptorist community, such as Kevin Dowling, now Bishop of Rustenberg, Anthony Padua, Peter Robb, and Michael Fish (now a Camaldolese monk), in the Provinces of South Africa, in Australia and in Baltimore, USA, have also played a very important part in my life story. I am indebted to them.

Prologue

My mother gazed at the picture for a few moments, then quickly turned away. There were tears rolling down her wrinkled old cheeks. I leant towards her. She turned slowly to face me and told me how to her, as a good Jewess, it really was a mystery to have a Catholic priest for a son.

It was in the late summer of 1973, just a year before she passed peacefully away. I remember sitting quietly with her in the living room of her house in Parktown North, one of the northern suburbs of Johannesburg. She sat in front of the fireplace in her favourite armchair while I sat on the sofa nearby. On the wall hung the large black-and-white photograph of me wearing my Roman cassock as a newly ordained priest, a gold embossed Bible in my hand.

It was then that she spoke of commissioning someone to write a book about my life, a life that she felt must be unique among both Jews and Catholics. I just shook my head wistfully, a sign I think of the inner conflict that I still had about my faith. She never told anyone else of her wish and eventually gave up trying to persuade me, but that moment, as we sat together, she had planted the seed.

My mother was not the first person to suggest that my story should be written down. My kindly school Principal, Sister Thomasia, who kept in touch with me long after I left St Vincent's School for the Deaf in Johannesburg, also intermittently suggested that my story was worth telling. She had followed with interest my progress and my struggles at theological college in Pretoria where, as the first deaf person to train for the priesthood, I had been allowed to study alone and find my own way to learn. She herself penned an article about my experiences there and later suggested that I should use it as a starting point for something more substantial.

Many years afterwards, in 1985, when I was doing pastoral work in the Johannesburg area, the article re-surfaced. It was found by an Irish Dominican nun whose loyalty and commitment was exceptional, and who was my personal assistant at the time. Having found it, Sister Mannes also began secretly collecting newspaper cuttings and notes about my work. In 1995 when she died, the collected papers could not be found. That did not matter because deep in my memory the stories and events were far from lost.

The dedication that others had put into preserving samples of my life and work touched me and were soon to become the springboard from which my determination to tell my own story grew. It had been a story too painful to tell earlier because of the wrenching spiritual journey I had made as a young man, and later because of the earth-shattering discovery that as a deaf man in his forties I was now to lose my sight.

My resolve was renewed when, in 1996, I was escorting a small group of Chinese deaf people on a trip to the world's only University solely for deaf people, Gallaudet University, Washington DC. It was an emotional time, as I was enabling my colleagues to learn the leadership skills that they would take back to their own community in Macau.

However, I suddenly found myself stranded when I developed a thrombosis in my right leg. The American doctors advised me not to return to Macau until I had fully recovered. Taking their advice, I stayed on in a community house for Redemptorists, my own religious order, at the Holy Redeemer College. Dr Jack Gannon, the author of the classic book *Deaf Heritage: A Narrative History of Deaf America (1981)*, visited me. He persuaded me that I had waited long enough and that now was the right time for the seeds in my soul to germinate, and for my story to be offered to the public. So there, in the quiet basement room of the library, I used my period of convalescence to reflect, to gather my thoughts and recollections and to set to work on writing them down.

It was to be a huge challenge. How was I going to write a book? As a born-deaf person, I lacked confidence in my written English, and I did not even know whether my sight would hold up long enough for me to see to type the manuscript?

I thought about commissioning a biographer as my mother had suggested, but I wanted my own voice to be heard. I took advice. Jack Gannon gave me guidance about how to compile a book. My South African godfather, Dr Robert Simmons, who was working as a temporary lecturer at

Gallaudet University at the time, gave me the encouragement I needed to overcome my inhibitions and follow my inner instinct to write. He reassured me that if I needed assistance with the English he would help me and if my eyesight gave out I could dictate to him in sign language and he would prepare a written draft. Since then, I have become completely blind and without his help this book would never have been written, and my mother's wish that my life be known to the world, would never have been fulfilled.

For the last three years my publisher's editor, who is a fluent sign language user, my interpreter/guide and I have worked together tirelessly, using a mixture of tactile sign language, fingerspelling on to the palm of my hand and Braille, through which I can access my computer and emails. It has been a long and painstaking exercise, involving practically daily email exchange and much travelling.

Finally my story is told. To me, my life has been like a mystery that has gradually unfolded. My mother planted the tiny seeds in my soul that have grown as I have made my many journeys through life. These have been journeys of faith, of life, of work, travelled at different times and in many parts of the world.

I believe that every human individual has within them their own unique and interesting story to tell. So I have written this book about my life to give thanks to all who have encouraged me along the way but also as a token of appreciation for God's boundless love and faith in me that has so enriched my heart and given me courage.

I do hope that this book will help people understand my journeys and be of interest to them whatever their faith or

beliefs. I hope too that it might be a source of encouragement and enlightenment to others as they make their own
journeys through life.

CHAPTER ONE

The Right Moment

There I was in my sixtieth year standing on the stage, once again in the vast hall of Gallaudet University, Washington DC, when I became aware that the audience of over a thousand had erupted into applause. They were not clapping but stamping their feet and shouting congratulations and support to me. On and on it went, for over a minute, the air tingling around my face, the vibrations felt through my feet and through my body. I could not hear, I could not see, for now I was completely deafblind, but my heart heard the applause and sensed the audience's delight as the President of the university took my left hand and raised it into the air for the long ovation.

The Honorary Doctorate that I was receiving was in recognition of my thirty-eight years of service to deaf people in my native South Africa and in South East Asia. It was a memorable experience and meant more than I can say.

A few months earlier I had been sitting in my room at Rainbow Court at Deafblind UK in Peterborough, England. It had been the darkest of times for me. I felt that, as my sight closed in, my life was being taken away from me. How could I continue my priesthood? How could I continue my service to deaf people? Then, I received this wonderful surprise, the email letter from President I. King Jordan to say that I had been selected to receive an honorary doctorate.

As a deafblind person, getting myself over to the USA was not simple and required a huge amount of planning. The day of travel – 8 May 2001 – arrived, and I was taken by taxi to Heathrow Airport. Once I was there, Virgin Atlantic Airways were wonderful in meeting my special needs. I was escorted onto the plane and was given my own stewardess to assist me during the flight. She informed me that her brother was deaf and her sister was blind and I found that she knew some British Sign Language and also the deafblind manual alphabet, so she was able to communicate with me by spelling out words on my hand.

At Dulles Airport in Washington DC she escorted me to the meeting area where an American Sign Language inter-preter, who was deaf himself, was waiting for me. He and another deaf person had been appointed by the university to assist me while I was there. For two days I underwent a crash course in Tactile American Sign Language. I already knew American Sign Language from when I had my sight, and studied in the USA, but to learn how to receive it through feeling the signer's hands (Hands-on Signing) was really

7

difficult and especially picking up the one-handed finger-spelling through touch. In England the Tactile British Sign Language and two-handed fingerspelling that I was used to was quite different, but with plenty of practice I soon picked it up.

My cousin Dawn, who over the years has become the dearest of friends to me – and the family member with whom I have the deepest bond - flew in from South Africa. She accompanied me to a dinner the evening before the ceremony hosted by the President of the university and his wife. I was introduced to members of the Board of Trustees and the Council and other VIPs.

How different it was from when I was a student at Gallaudet in the 1960s. For now the President was a deaf man and most of the professors were deaf. When I was there as a young man the teaching was excellent and it equipped deaf people for life in a hearing world. However, it was not by deaf people as it is today. In those days sign languages were not widely recognized as proper languages with their own grammar and syntax; deaf culture and deaf history were not talked about.

Next day, Dawn and I attended a lavish pre-ceremony lunch joined by other friends and colleagues, including a remarkable Chinese deaf woman Alice Lao Iok Ieng, with whom I used to work and who had travelled with her husband all the way from Macau. I was also surprised and delighted to meet many of my old university teachers. It was very moving for me.

The graduation ceremony followed. Dressed in a black gown and mortarboard, I was guided by my two interpreters as we joined the procession of academics in their full regalia into the hall. My interpreters described the layout of the vast hall for me, where large projector screens had been placed above and to the side of the stage to enable the entire deaf audience to follow the proceedings. I was guided to my seat in the centre of the stage. After the opening speeches, the Chairman of the Board of Trustees read a citation. I stood with my interpreters either side of me, and with two deaf representatives from South Africa and China behind me. The President then bestowed on me the Honorary Doctorate of Laws as he laid the purple collar with yellow stripes around my shoulders and presented me with the certificate and citation. It was then that the applause started.

I was overwhelmed but it seemed to me that the honour that I was receiving belonged not to me but to all the deaf people in South Africa and China who placed their confidence and trust in my simple abilities to develop services for and with them. I also felt that the honour had come to me at just the right moment in my life. It came as fresh hope and gave me the challenge I needed. It made me appreciate that my blindness could never take away my life's work from me, and that the blindness itself would, from that moment on, become another contribution I could make to the world. At that moment I reflected on my life and everything seemed to come together. My Jewish family, confrères of the Redemptorist order, my friends, deaf and deafblind, from South Africa, from Hong Kong and from the USA - all were there in the audience. All had been with me in different ways on the many journeys of life and faith that God had so far chosen for me.

CHAPTER TWO

My Jewish Parents

My parents were both brought up in Orthodox Jewish families in Eastern Europe. It was a time when Jewish people suffered from dreadful oppression and from the pogroms of the Tsar and Eastern European governments. At that time Jews were regarded as outsiders, with no privileges of citizenship or civil status, and thousands were fleeing the ghettos and villages to seek a better life elsewhere.

My father, Abe Axelrod, was born Abelis Akselrodaski in the late 1890s into the rabbinical circle in Vilna, a small town in Poland. His family were poor and their lifestyle was very simple, rather like that portrayed in the musical *Fiddler on the Roof.* Although they did not have material wealth, they had a religious life that was very rich and very orthodox. My father's father was a rabbi and spent much of his time reading and discussing the Talmud. He was well known and respected for his knowledge and he passed much of it on to his son.

Abe wanted to follow in his father's footsteps and become a rabbi, but with the outbreak of the First World War he had to abandon that idea and instead he set off for South Africa in search of a better life. At first he worked in a butcher's shop in a small town outside Johannesburg and then as a storeroom manager for a wholesale company in the city.

He quickly became well known to local rabbis in Johannesburg and it was not long before the Chief Rabbi was inviting him to share his knowledge with others on the Sabbath.

My mother, Yetta Goodman – born Eta Gutman – was raised in a large family in Seduva, Lithuania. She was the second youngest of nine children, two of whom died in infancy. Her family were comfortably off. They ran a large shop that sold woollen goods, which were in high demand in the cold Lithuanian winters. They too were Orthodox Jews and her mother, Shifre, taught my mother to read the Psalms in Hebrew.

In the 1890s, before my mother was born, her three older brothers had already left home to join the gold rush in South Africa. Her father had gone with them initially, and hoped that later the whole family would move there. However, his Orthodox Jewish observance made it difficult for him to accept that businesses were trading on the Sabbath, and he returned to Lithuania, where he died in 1919.

A few years later my mother's younger brother, Oscar, joined the other brothers in South Africa and so did her sister, May.

Later, as Nazism, and anti-Semitism, spread from Germany into Eastern Europe and just before it reached Lithuania in 1931, Yetta and my maternal grandmother, like so many others, decided to flee, leaving only one sister who eventually settled in Moscow. My mother and grandmother started to make plans to join the others in South Africa. Although it was forbidden to take valuables out of the country, they managed to save some of their heirlooms. They hid lace curtains, cut glass, and bone china in their large cabin trunks. They put their silver in boxes of coal; for passengers needed their own coal to burn in their cabin fireplace to keep warm on the ship. My mother and grandmother abandoned their home and their shop and set out on the long sea voyage.

There, in Johannesburg, my mother and father met. In 1937, already well into their forties, the marriage of Yetta Goodman and Abe Axelrod took place at the city's Berea Synagogue.

CHAPTER THREE

My Early Years

For the five years after their marriage, Abe and Yetta longed for a child. According to the Mosaic Law, parents should have a child in order to fulfil God's covenant with Abraham that his progeny would multiply like the stars in heaven. Just after midnight on 24 February 1942, my mother gave birth to a boy.

Eight days after my birth the rite of circumcision, *Bris*, was performed with great ceremony in the presence of my assembled family in our small apartment. At the ceremony, I was given the Hebrew name Sheftil ben Avram Abba. Sheftil was my maternal grandmother's family name and as my grandfather, Abe, had been a rabbi, it was also a great honour to have 'ben Avram Abba', 'Son of Father Abraham', in my name. Unfortunately, when my father tried to register me under this name, the South African Birth Registry refused to accept it because it was not 'English' enough. So my parents decided to register me under the name Cyril, after Prince Cyril of Russia, brother of Tsar Nicholas II.

I was a frail and unresponsive baby and as the months went by my parents began to feel anxious. They could see that my physical and my mental development were slow but they had no idea why. Doubts began to creep into their hearts and eventually they shared their concerns with my mother's eldest sister, my Aunt May. One day when we visited her, she noticed that I was showing no signs of learning to walk and she urged my parents to take me to the doctor to find out what was wrong with me. Eventually, I was taken to the children's hospital for physiotherapy. There, with the help of arm bars, I learned to walk. On the last day, my parents stood at the front door of the hospital and, with tears in their eyes, watched me struggling to walk independently towards them. My parents were most relieved that I was now starting to make progress but they still did not understand the cause of my unresponsiveness - and *my* struggles were only just beginning.

My parents could barely speak English. Their mother tongue was Yiddish and this was what they used with me but I did not respond. A fresh anxiety gripped them and my mother, in her distress, turned again to the support of her eldest sister. From this time on, my dear Aunt May became one of the most important people in my early life, and it was she who arranged for me to see a hospital specialist for an ear examination when I was three. I was taken into the consulting room, together with my mother, my father, Aunt

May and her daughter Beulah, who was then about nineteen years old. The door slammed loudly behind me but blissfully unaware, I continued to play happily with the toys on the floor. It was Beulah who commented that I had not responded to the sound. When the specialist confirmed that I was congenitally profoundly deaf and informed my parents that I would never hear, it was Aunt May who took me on her lap and held me close to her.

My parents' hopes and dreams were shattered. They knew nothing of deafness or what it would mean to have a deaf son. The doctor tried to reassure them, advising them that, even though I was so young, if I boarded for a while at a nearby Catholic school for the deaf, I would eventually learn to speak and write English. This was not much comfort, for my parents knew what it would mean. Having little English themselves, they knew that they would have difficulty in communicating with me and that the family language of Yiddish would not be my first language.

Their anguish was great; they had no idea what would become of me. They certainly could never have known that deafness was not the only disability that their son would eventually have to face. *My* first journey was just beginning.

At first, my parents were distressed by the idea of sending me to a Catholic school and turned instead to a private school for the deaf in Durban. They had heard that a wealthy family who had a deaf child had established this school and had hired a governess from Scotland to run it. However, it had not succeeded and had closed down. So they had no choice after all but to send me to St Vincent's School in Johannesburg, which had been run by German

15

Dominican sisters since 1934.

Still only three years old, I was enrolled as a weekly boarder into the nursery school. Straight away I was given intensive speech training and this training was to remain a major part of my schooling for the next five years. Even so, I was nine before I could pronounce the words 'Mummy' and 'Daddy' and then my speech was barely more than a mumble. It was even longer before I could speak in sentences.

My parents found this period very distressing. I think of them as my 'silent' years. They were years when I watched and observed and during which I developed a kind of sixth sense, an intuition, and slowly began to make sense of the world around me.

I remember that even as Aunt May held me close on her lap when my deafness was being diagnosed, a strange feeling came upon me as I observed the anguish on my parents' faces. Even at such a young age I was aware of their sadness. For the next five years I watched them as they spoke to each other, wondering what it was that they said. When I met other family members, I would watch their faces and see their emotions even though they could not communicate with me. I would see a loving gesture, a sympathetic eye, a smile, and feel their love and affection - and that was enough for me.

I would sit by my father as he listened to the radio, watching his face and wondering what his enjoyment could possibly be. Once, I moved towards that old-fashioned wireless and stretched my hand out to touch it. I felt the vibrations and knew that this was sound but had no real means of knowing what it was. For me, deafness was not a source of pain or loss, for I had known it all my life. Sound *was* a source of curiosity though. I tried to get my father's attention by tapping on his leg because I wanted him to know that I could feel the sound and I wanted to know what it was he was listening to. I could not make myself understood and he gently put me back on my chair, putting his forefinger to his lips. I knew he was telling me to be quiet and so my curiosity about the meaning of sound and the meaning of silence remained my private wonder. It was the mystery of my life in the silence of my world. Bit by bit, and by myself, I pieced together my awareness of the world and what was happening around me. I learned what it was to be deaf and I slowly accepted it as part of me.

Although I could not know the tones of speech and even though the gap of communication was huge, I instinctively knew my parents' love for me. I could not understand their words but I knew how helpless they felt. I knew how much they wanted to communicate with me and how hard they tried to help me understand them. Even as a child I developed a sensitivity and sympathy for the inadequacy that they felt. It is amazing that their struggle to communicate with me and to cope with my deafness was an example of love and service without words. This, and my parents' religious practice, had already given me sight of God within them and would later motivate me in service to others. They showed me that there can be communication without words and to me this was something beautiful, like God.

I think I was fortunate. The love I received from my family somehow cushioned the lack of verbal communication between us and made it easier for me years later to forgive my parents for their limitations. Many of my deaf contemporaries never experienced that and grew up to feel resentful and damaged by the difficulties in communication that they had had with their families.

At that time parents were not encouraged to use sign language with their deaf children, as lipreading and speech were the preferred methods. As an adult, my pastoral work would teach me how much some deaf people have suffered as a result of this and many times I have found myself counselling others in forgiveness.

However, as a small child I too had many difficulties. I was a sensitive and nervous child, and at school I was often bullied or picked on by other children. It is difficult to put my finger on the reason for this, but from the beginning, I felt different from other deaf children. I felt clumsy and sometimes isolated in their company. I found it particularly hard to express how I felt, partly because of communication difficulties but partly because my parents could not share their feelings with me either. Instead, I was rather withdrawn. I preferred to watch from the sidelines and because of this other people often considered me a mysterious child. Already as a young boy, I was developing a resilience and a quiet acceptance of adversity that would allow me to face whatever life would throw at me without bitterness or anger. What I did not know then was that there were other things already affecting me - my sight, which must by then have been less than perfect, and my poor balance. It would be almost another thirty years before these things would become clear to me.

My difficulties with communication also came out in my behaviour at home. From time to time I would deliberately break an ornament or tear up papers or even a precious photograph. It was sheer frustration that I felt, rather than defiance or anger. This was the only way I could communicate my distress. My parents would reprimand me with a warning slap on the leg, but I knew that they felt inadequate because they could not reason with me or help me to understand my behaviour. They would move things out of my reach and, not understanding or being understood, I would stamp my feet in rage.

Once, when I was seven, while my parents were in the kitchen washing up after our Friday night meal, I gazed at the lighted candles left on the sideboard in the dining room and I was entranced by the dancing flames. I took the candlesticks and placed them on the windowsill behind the lace curtains and close to the heavy velvet drapes that hung in front of them. The lace caught fire and I watched with delight the beauty of the flames as the fire took hold. Immediately someone came to the front door and told my parents. They rushed into the room, pulled down the curtains and extinguished the fire. Instinctively, my father slapped my leg again, not knowing how to explain the danger of fire to me. My mother stood by and wept tears of despair. They both wanted so much to be able to communicate with me. My father then took me to the kitchen and held my hand above the stove until it became so hot that I pulled it away. At that moment, I had learned the danger of fire and it was one of the first things I learned from my father without speech or sign.

Soon after this, my father enrolled at night school to study English so he could communicate with me better. Meanwhile at school, I was picking up sign language from the other children in the playground, and benefiting from the stimulation and motivation this gave me. For the first time I could fully understand what people were talking about and I could share my feelings and thoughts with others. The ease and companionship I felt with my deaf peer group was to become important to me throughout my life. Later, my father also learned to use both British finger-spelling and some sign language in order to build a basic vocabulary for daily communication between us. Even so, communication with my parents remained very difficult for me.

But their main fear while I was at school was that I might become influenced by the Catholic teaching. So they asked the Principal to exempt me from attending the religious classes. They hoped that I would still keep my strict Jewish faith although, sadly, they knew that they were not capable of instructing me in it themselves. Sister Thomasia responded with her usual kind wisdom. She realised how important it was to my parents and offered to arrange for me to learn about the 'God of Israel' at school.

And so it was that my relationships with those wonderful teachers, the German Dominican nuns, became deeper. They began to supplement the speech training with finger-spelling that in time helped me to learn to use my voice. As I grew closer and closer to my Catholic teachers, my Jewish parents became more and more concerned, but this was only a small taste of what was to come.

1. My maternal grandfather, Abraham Goodman.

2. My maternal grandmother, Shifre Goldberg.

3. My maternal grandparents' shop in Lithuania.

4. My mother, Yetta Goodman.

5. My father, Abe Axelrod, at work in Johannesburg.

6. My mother and father on their honeymoon in Durban, 1937.

7. Aged one with our dog Lucky, 1943.

8. Aged two with my mother. I was still unable to walk.

9. Aged three, just after the diagnosis of my profound deafness.

CHAPTER FOUR

The Rosary

It seems strange that a rosary, the string of beads that represents the sacred beliefs and prayers of the Catholic religion, should have had such importance to me as a young Jewish boy. What happened has always seemed amazing to me.

Two places – the Catholic school and the Jewish home – made me aware of the differences between the two religions, but my young mind could not really comprehend these differences. My father always tried to explain to me that we were just humble and ordinary Jews, but this was a concept beyond my understanding.

One Friday when I was nine years old, when my father fetched me home from school for the weekend, he took off my school jacket and emptied my pockets and there he found a small green leather purse containing a small jade rosary. Startled and upset, he asked me what it was doing there. I did not know. I tried to convey to him that I thought someone must have put it in my pocket by mistake. It was an innocent answer but suspicion had already been aroused in my father's heart. He told my mother and she was also upset. 'What are we doing with our son? How can we teach him that we are Jews and not Catholics?' she asked my father. Again, I could sense their great fear for my future.

My father, who was always such a quiet and unassuming man, went to the school housemother and inquired how that rosary came to be in my pocket. She was very apologetic and asked him to return it to her. For some reason he decided to keep it. Why, remains a mystery to this day.

After this incident, Sister Thomasia and my father met together and decided that maybe I should not be boarding at the school. So it was that I became the first pupil to travel home after school every day. From then on, my parents insisted that I practise Judaism.

However, my father was still so worried that he went to address a large gathering of members of the Board of Jewish Deputies at the Jewish Orphanage in Johannesburg. I sat in the front row, next to a generous and loving friend of his, Ralph Hahn. I watched my father as he told the meeting that his son was at a Catholic school and was being influenced by the Catholic doctrine.

Even to my young eyes, it was apparent how upset and downhearted my gentle father was. He placed the rosary on the table in front of the Chief Rabbi, saying, 'How would you feel if your child had no access to the Jewish faith? I beg you to consider the possibility of educating my deaf son and

31

any other deaf Jewish children at his school in the Jewish faith.' The members, there and then, unanimously resolved to offer Jewish religious education at my school. They also agreed to establish a hostel for the deaf students whose parents lived too far away from the school for them to go home. The hostel would offer a proper Jewish upbringing and education out of school hours. The members also recognised that there was a need for a centre for Jewish deaf adults.

After negotiations with Sister Thomasia, the Board of Jewish Deputies appointed Ralph Hahn as our Hebrew teacher, the same man I had sat next to at the meeting. I remember him so well. Stout and warm-hearted, and always with a kind smile, Ralph Hahn was famous for his Peterson pipe that spread aromatic fragrance all around him. He had lost some hearing during the bombing in North Africa in 1940, and a year later had become involved with the deaf community, picking up sign language with remarkable speed. It was soon arranged for him to come into one of the class-rooms every day from Monday to Friday to teach the fifteen Jewish deaf pupils to read and write in Hebrew. We also read and recited the Hebrew prayer over bread and wine using the Roman alphabet. There were a few girls but most were boys and they wore their Jewish skullcaps during the class.

Three years later, in 1951, the hostel, comprising a social centre and sports recreation centre, was established in Parktown, an affluent area of Johannesburg where the Jewish stockbrokers had their large homes. The Society for the Welfare of the Jewish Deaf, it was called. It looked after twelve Jewish deaf children from my school and I used to join them after school for further Hebrew lessons.

I remember as a child going to the hostel every Sunday, a day of recreation, to meet the Jewish deaf adults there. There would be games of tennis and much chatting over tea and cake. The important festivals such as Passover and the Jewish New Year, Rosh Hashanah, were always celebrated there and were very well attended by deaf adults. Mr Hahn officiated at the ceremonies in sign language so that all of us, especially the young deaf Jews, could fully participate in the religious experience.

It seems to me that the discovery of the rosary in my pocket all those years before really was of great significance. It raised such sensitive issues for my parents and for the Jewish people in their circle. Jews do not usually discuss their faith with non-Jews, whom they call 'goyim', but here because of the rosary, they were organising special Jewish teaching in a Catholic school. If the rosary had not appeared in my pocket my parents would probably have sent me to England or Israel for a good Jewish education.

It is still a mystery to me how much the rosary has meant and how in some ways it has guided me through different phases of my life without my even realising it. I never did learn why my father kept it so safe in the green leather pouch for all those years. It was not until after his death from stomach cancer in 1961, when he was sixty-eight, that it was discovered there by my mother. She then kept it herself right up to her death thirteen years later. Now it is with me here in England, and although both my parents lie buried in the Jewish cemetery in Johannesburg, I continue to marvel at how that Catholic rosary has influenced my life and theirs.

CHAPTER FIVE

My Jewish Life

The Jewish way of life and faith, with its innumerable symbols and meanings, can be difficult to explain. I hope that by sharing my personal experiences they will become clearer.

When I was just a year old, we moved out of the one-bedroom apartment where I was born, into a house in the same neighbourhood. My mother's three brothers had become successful businessmen, and had set up companies dealing in gold, diamonds and property. As a very generous wedding present they had given my parents enough money to buy and furnish a comfortable six-bedroom house.

The two-storey, red and white brick house, with a red tiled roof, stood in a quarter of an acre with a large lawn at the front. Built in 1915, it had a large balcony that I thought made it look very grand.

However, Berea was a working-class Jewish neighbour-hood in the northern outskirts of Johannesburg, and my parents were hard-working Jewish folk. They lived a quiet life there among the many Orthodox and Hasidic Jews and my father had an ordinary job as a store-man working hard to support his wife and young child. To make ends meet, they let the six bedrooms in the house out for bed-and-breakfast for Jewish people so my parents and I had to sleep down-stairs.

My mother devoted herself to the simple Jewish life, looking after me, preparing kosher food for the family, read-ing the Psalms in Hebrew every day and observing the Jewish laws. All the important Jewish festivals were strictly observed in our household and it was then that the precious family heirlooms from Lithuania, the silver, the china and the cut glass, were brought out.

Every week the large dining room became the focus for our Friday night celebrations when we honoured the Sabbath, sometimes called the 'heart of all Jewish-ness'. The Sabbath commences on Friday evening with a family meal at which blessings are said over wine and bread, called the Kiddush, and ends on Saturday evening when the first three stars appear in the sky. The dining room was large enough for the massive, dark wood dining table, with six leather chairs around it, which stood on a big, rectangular, red Persian carpet with wide white fringes at both ends. Red velvet curtains hung from the ceiling to the wooden floor to cover the large windows. Above the dining table, a decora-tive brass lamp with small candle bulbs hung from the plain white ceiling.

To the right of the dining table was a large sideboard in which the bone china crockery, sterling silver and crystal-cut wine glasses were kept especially for the Sabbath. On top of the sideboard was a hot plate from which food was placed into the silver dishes.

To the left hung a large, thick-framed, black-and-white photograph of my maternal grandmother, Shifre. She had a stern and stony face and her hair wound into a tight bun on the back of her head. She wore a high-necked black dress with handmade lace over her shoulders. Several fine gold chains hung around her neck and a pair of gold-rimmed spectacles rested on her chest. But her severe face had the hint of a serene smile. It was as if she presided over the table, and looked on with approval at our Sabbath celebrations.

On the table stood two large handmade silver candlesticks entwined with silver moulded grapes and leaves. Near to the chair where my father sat as head of the family was a silver Kiddush cup engraved in Hebrew with the words *Shema Yisroel Adonai Elohanou Adonai Echad* (Hear, O Israel. The Lord our God, the Lord is One) and in it there was sweet red wine.

The special plaited Challah bread was covered with a white silk cloth embroidered with a dark blue Star of David. The crockery, with floral design, was placed on the table together with beautifully carved cutlery and crystal wine glasses laid for three people – my father, my mother and me.

From my earliest infancy onwards, at sunset, just before the ceremony began, I would watch my mother place a black lace scarf over her head, light the two large beeswax candles and say a prayer over them. I stood beside her wondering what it all meant. She looked at me silently, not knowing how to explain to her deaf child, but her actions alone gave me a significant experience of a faith in God. This I could understand in my childlike way.

She would then place silver dishes of chopped herring or liver, lamb chops and a selection of vegetables and also a large silver bowl of chicken broth on the white linen table-cloth. The fragrant aroma of the kosher food permeated the dining room, and signified a blessing from God.

At the table, my father, with his skullcap on his head, would take me on his lap. He would point at the large silver goblet of red wine and the silk covered Challah. He would open the Hebrew prayer book and I would look at it without comprehension. And then my eyes would fix on his mouth mumbling a prayer that I could not hear, and I would watch his head rhythmically nodding over the book as he read.

This was the beginning of my awareness of Jewish life at home.

My mother observed the strict rules of Kashrut, which involve keeping separate those dishes used for dairy products and those for meat. She reprimanded me whenever I used the wrong linen cloth to dry the dishes – the red for meat dishes and the green for dairy.

Fixed on the right-hand doorpost of the front door was the mezuzah, a little oblong box containing a scroll of the Ten Commandments. Whenever we left the house or returned, my father would lift me up, instructing me to put my right hand on the mezuzah and then to put my hand on my mouth as if to kiss it. If my father was not there, I called my mother for help or I moved the chair to the door and climbed up on it myself.

When I was seven, I was taken out of school for a few days to celebrate Rosh Hashanah, the Jewish New Year. My father took me to the synagogue in Berea for the first time. The small upper prayer room fascinated me. Below the golden Star of David hung a white velvet curtain with white silk appliqué. On the silk there was gold embroidery of the Ten Commandments in Hebrew with a crown above and a Lion of Judea on each side. Behind the curtain was the Ark of the Covenant, where several scrolls of the Torah - the five books of Moses from the Old Testament - were kept safely.

The men, wearing either hats or white and blue skullcaps, sat on the right side, while the women wearing their best dresses and hats were on the left. They all sat praying towards the Ark of the Covenant. I was entranced. My father smiled at me and I knew he was trying to communicate something important. Watching his lips and gestures I understood his message. 'This is the place where you belong and pray to God.' I nodded and, even as a small child, I already realised that my Jewish identity was quite different from the faith that was practised at my Catholic school.

In 1952, when I was ten, my Hebrew teacher, Mr. Hahn, introduced me for the first time to the Great Synagogue, a red brick building whose interior and exterior fascinated me too. He took me there one Sabbath and I remember that visit well.

The marble surround of the Ark of the Covenant was decorated in gold, red and blue, and I could not take my eyes off the exquisitely embroidered white and gold curtain. On each side of the Ark stood a large brass menorah with electric, candle-shaped lights, and on the right was the dark wooden prayer seat of the Chief Rabbi. Opposite the Ark of the Covenant was the bimah, an elevated desk, which seemed huge to me, where the Chief Cantor sang the psalms and prayers, and below it were three black leather seats that I learned were for the President, and for the Senior and Junior Wardens. On both sides of the synagogue several rows of dark, polished wooden seats faced each other. These were reserved for the men, while in this synagogue the women sat in the semi-circular balcony upstairs. In the centre of the building, the light blue ceiling was domed and displayed a Star of David in gold, from which hung a large brass chandelier. In this building I felt a sense of awe. I was enthralled by the beauty of the place and the special atmosphere began to make me realise for the first time what it meant to be Jewish.

After that, I regularly attended the Synagogue on Fridays and Saturdays with Mr Hahn and other Jewish pupils from the school. Although Orthodox Jewish people are not permitted to travel by bus or car to the synagogue on the Sabbath, Mr Hahn got special permission from the Chief Rabbi to take us by car. It was the only way we could get there. Inside the synagogue, Mr Hahn instructed the deaf boys how to use the skullcap and tallith (the prayer shawl) with reverence, while the deaf girls prayed in the upper balcony. As Jewish worship involves meaningful participation, despite my deafness, I quickly found myself following the readings of the Torah and joining in with the chant at the

39

closing of the Ark of the Covenant. As the Chief Rabbi and the Cantor sang the Shema, 'Hear, O Israel. The Lord our God, the Lord is One', and the curtains of the Ark of the Covenant closed, I found it a profoundly uplifting religious experience, even at the tender age of ten.

By the time I was eleven, my parents and I had moved again. They had been approached by the council and asked to sell our house and land. Private developers wanted to build apartments there and were offering five times the original purchase price. My mother and father saw this as an opportunity to move to Hillbrow, at that time a middle-class area a few miles from the centre of town. All they could afford there was a one-bedroom apartment, and so for the next four years I shared their bedroom, with only a wardrobe separating my bed from theirs. They still had a very modest income and continued to live their simple, honest, Jewish life.

Before long it was time for my Bar Mitzvah - the religious rite by which a Jewish boy is formally initiated into the religious community and assumes the duties and responsibilities of a Jew. There are three parts to a Bar Mitzvah. First I would have to read from the Torah in public. Then I must profess my faith and finally I must assume my responsibilities to live a life of Jewish observance.

I was so lucky to have Mr Hahn as my instructor. He understood my deafness and he had so patiently taught us at school the Hebrew alphabet and then the Hebrew vocabulary, by writing Hebrew and English words side by side. Now he started to prepare me in the portion that I would have to read. Going over it again and again, I understood and learned the Hebrew by heart. On the day of my Bar Mitzvah I felt so privileged when I was called up to the reading desk wearing my skullcap and prayer shawl; a young deaf Jewish boy being initiated from childhood into adulthood.

I felt nervous as I looked closely for the very first time at the Torah that had been taken out of the Ark of the Covenant for the service. As part of the ritual, holding the four corners of my prayer shawl, where the knotted tassels represented the Ten Commandments, I carefully placed them on the Torah and then kissed them. Then I started to read aloud the opening prayer before reading from the Torah in public for the very first time.

After reciting my portion and a closing blessing I went back to my seat. Then Ralph Hahn interpreted in sign language as, from the high pulpit, the Chief Rabbi gave a sermon about reaching the age of faith. The Chief Rabbi then brought me back to the reading desk and blessed me by placing his hands on my head. At this moment, the congregation began solemnly to applaud me. I could not hear them, of course, but saw their pride in me and it was a wonderful moment. There was such a community spirit in the Synagogue. My dear father embraced me in congratulation. I then went up to the women's gallery where my mother stood with other female relatives. Still barely able to communicate with her deaf son, my mother wept in an unspoken gesture of emotion and gave me a gentle kiss. My poor mother had found it so hard to bring up a deaf child and so difficult to accept my deafness. On that day, when I became an adult, she must have had such mixed emotions. She said not a word, but the expression on her face was communication quite eloquent enough for me.

On reflection, it now seems incredible how I had emerged from my 'silent years' when as a young deaf child I had understood so little. It had been largely thanks to the sheer determination of my school Principal and the other dedicated teachers who believed in me and in my ability to learn. Indeed, they believed passionately that all deaf children should be given the confidence to fulfil their potential.

A year after my Bar Mitzvah, Ralph Hahn suddenly died. He had given so much to Jewish deaf people and we held him in great affection and esteem. He was greatly respected and acclaimed in Jewish circles but within the Johannesburg deaf community his passing left a huge void, unfilled to this day. After his death the practice of the Jewish faith by deaf people fell into disarray. They were like lost sheep without their shepherd.

However, I continued to attend the regular worship on Fridays and Saturdays. I was sometimes called to read from the Torah or to close it after the reading session. I regarded that as a very special privilege that made me feel close to God.

The more the Sabbath observance intrigued me, the more involved I became in Jewish youth activities, such as religious studies of the Talmud, dancing and sport. Now that Mr Hahn was no longer alive, I had to start getting used to integrating with the non-deaf young Jewish people. I was the only deaf person there. With the help of typed notes given to me by the rabbi, I was able to join their study circle. Communication was not easy but using a mixture of written notes, gesture and lipreading, I was determined to learn more about the teaching of the Early Fathers.

I think my general thirst for learning began around this time. I was particularly interested in people's lives and I loved my visits to the public library where I read biographies and discovered the classics. For now at last I was beginning to develop the ability to understand abstract ideas and I had a hungry appetite for learning through books.

It was not until much later, after I left school, that I began to get to grips with writing English myself. For learning the grammar and idioms of a language that one had never heard was to be a big challenge for me, as it is for many born deaf people. That would be where Gallaudet University in the USA would come to my rescue.

43

CHAPTER SIX

Holy Days

During the four years that we lived in the Hillbrow apartment, my father's hard work was rewarded with promotion to Store Manager. This meant that we could move to somewhere bigger. So when I was fifteen we found a two-bedroom apartment in Parktown, which was a more affluent area, further north again, where many Jewish businesspeople lived.

Every Saturday morning I waited outside for the Chief Rabbi who passed on his way to the Great Synagogue. Wearing his black suit and hat, he would greet me, *'Shabbat Shalom'* ('Peace on the Sabbath'), and I would join him on the two-mile walk to *shul* (synagogue). As we walked he would try to give me a brief summary of the sermon that he was about to preach. He found it difficult to speak slowly and I struggled to lipread him through his beard – usually grasping only part of what he told me. But he was so keen to help me understand, that before we entered the congregational prayer hall, he would also show me the Torah reading for the day. After the service I walked home with him again.

One day, my mother told me that keeping food kosher was more important than going to the synagogue. It astonished me to think that any Jewish law could be more important than going to shul. So I asked Chief Rabbi Rabinowitz as we walked along. He thought for a moment, and then agreed that keeping food kosher *was* the most important Jewish observance. Over time, and through his great patience and perseverance, he taught me much great Jewish wisdom and the more I learned from him, the more intrigued I became with strict Orthodox Judaism. I slowly began to understand the meaning of all the Jewish festivals that my parents so strictly observed.

Sometimes, in the afternoon, I would walk the three blocks down from our apartment to the Chief Rabbi's home to study the Talmud and *Ethics of the Fathers* with a small group of Jewish youngsters. For me, every Saturday became a beautiful and enriching Jewish occasion.

As the Sabbath day came to an end, and we had observed the virtue of patience and respect all day, the young people would go outside to look for the three stars that signified that the day of rest was over. Immediately, we would start to socialise, jumping on the bus to go to a cinema or a restaurant or a cafe. Most of all we just wanted to be together at the end of the Sabbath.

An important family occasion for me was the celebratory Passover meal, which was quite different from the Friday night meal. Seder night is the first night of Passover, the eight-day Festival of Unleavened Bread. I remember coming to understand that this celebrated the freeing of the Jewish people as they fled into the desert from the slavery of the Egyptians.

The first part of the ceremony was very solemn and respectful. Our table was laden with the special crockery and cutlery that had to be used for Passover. Normally, they were stored away in boxes, wrapped carefully in old newspaper. I would help my mother unpack them and lay the table.

There was a plate of symbolic foods and I began to realise that the dish of bitter herbs in the centre of the table symbolised the slavery of the Jews in Egypt. The *matzos* carefully placed between layers of special Passover silk cloth represented the unleavened bread that my Jewish ancestors had so hurriedly taken with them. I was also fascinated by all the other Passover delicacies that were laid out along with the dried fruit and nuts on the sideboard.

We would sit at the table, my father and I in our skull-caps and my mother in a dark dress with a scarf on her head. When I was younger my father would take me on his knee as he rocked back and forth chanting from the Haggadah, the special book containing the Seder service. He would then take my hands in his as he clapped rhythmically.

Traditionally the youngest son in the family would recite the Ma Nishtanah, four questions about the meaning of all these symbols. As an only child, as soon as I was able, it became my privilege to do this and so become more fully involved in the ceremony.

My father would answer the questions and then the mood would change. He would sing the joyful song *Let us build a New Jerusalem,* and he would clap his hands to the rhythm. Although I could not hear him singing I could experience with him the joy of liberation for Jewish people.

Other ceremonies were quite different. There was the happy welcoming in of the Jewish New Year, Rosh Hashanah, celebrated both at home and at the synagogue. Ten days later there was Yom Kippur, the Day of Atonement. That involved a twenty-four-hour fast, beginning with a long evening service when the men wore black evening suits with bow ties and the women wore long dresses, fur coats and dazzling jewels.

Next day my father and I would pray from morning to evening in the synagogue and I remember how puzzled I was the first time that I was not allowed to eat or drink all day. I must have been about seven years old at the time but somehow or other my father managed to get the message across to me that I must pray for the forgiveness of my sins until evening came. It was a simple but beautiful experience.

In contrast to the fasting of Yom Kippur, the Feast of the Pentecost was a feast of food when fruit would be hung outside from a wooden arbour whose open roof was strewn with palm, willow branches and myrtle. The air was full of the fragrance of the fresh fruit and salads laid out on the table beneath.

Another memorable event happened later, when at seventeen I participated in a very rarely performed ceremony. It was the occasion of the consecrating of the Little Synagogue. This was a new building in the garden of the Great Synagogue that

47

was designated especially for use by the younger members of the congregation.

As is the custom when a new synagogue is built, a new Torah was bought. The first letters of the first names of all the young men were inscribed by an expert calligrapher on the last page. So *shin*, the first Hebrew letter of my name Sheftil, was inscribed. The Chief Rabbi placed his right hand on my head and blessed me. It was a wonderful moment.

When the inscriptions were finished the Torah was carefully closed, wrapped and knotted with a band of white cloth and finally covered with heavy red velvet embroidered with the Ten Commandments in Hebrew. Four of us were chosen to be bearers of a special canopy that was held over the rabbi as he carried the Torah in a procession out of the Great Synagogue and into the Little Synagogue where it was officially placed in the empty Ark of the Covenant. After psalms and prayers the Ark was closed and we danced in the garden outside.

10. Aunt May and Uncle Oscar, my mother's brother and sister.

11. Aged seven with my mother and father.

12. The Rosary.

13. Jewish deaf children with our Hebrew teacher, Ralph Hahn.
I am the second from the right in the front row, sucking a sweet.

14. Aged thirteen with my father after my Bar Mitzvah.

15. A concert at the Jewish Deaf Hostel to celebrate the Jewish Festival of Purim. I am wearing the crown, Johannesburg. 1954.

16. Celebrating Chanukah at the Jewish Deaf Hostel. I am fifteen and the tallest.

CHAPTER SEVEN

To Become a Rabbi?

When I was only fifteen, Abner Weiss, the young trainee rabbi of the Little Synagogue, unexpectedly invited me to join a small group who were considered suitable candidates for becoming rabbis. I was delighted and so were my parents.

First I had to attend a week-long study retreat at 'Shangri-la', a house outside Pretoria. There, Abner gave me one-to-one tuition in Jewish history, the Old Testament stories and the observance of laws. Unlike Ralph Hahn, he could not use sign language and most of our communication had to be written. There and then I decided I definitely wanted to become a rabbi, but two days before the end of the week my dreams were shattered. Abner had spoken to the Chief Rabbi who pointed out that according to the Laws of Moses, disabled people could not become rabbis; in fact they could even be exempted from Jewish observance altogether.

Even to this day, while the talents of deaf and disabled people have gained recognition, the interpretation of this law remains the subject of disagreement among Jewish legal authorities.

So Abner had to tell me that I could not become a rabbi after all. I was devastated and rushed outside in tears. I simply could not understand. I wanted to become a rabbi so much because I wanted to serve the Jewish deaf community in Johannesburg, and maybe later in Cape Town and Durban and other cities.

The Chief Rabbi came to comfort me. He was very gentle and very kind. However, because of his difficulty in communicating with me, he was unable to explain why I had been turned down. He did somehow manage to convey to me that God might have a different plan for me.

Despite my hurt and disappointment I accepted his wisdom although, at that stage, I had no idea that the rejection would eventually change the whole direction of my life. My poor parents felt guilty, especially my father. He probably knew all along that I would never be able to become a rabbi, but he had kept silent.

Nevertheless, this setback did not undermine my faith in Judaism. I continued to go to synagogue, but when I was there I found myself looking to the Ark of the Covenant, hoping for God's direction.

At home, I also became rather restless. My parents still led the simple life that they had known in their Eastern European upbringings. I wanted to broaden my horizons.

Sometime earlier I had been introduced to a well-educated

young Jewish woman with a gentle but lively personality. Valda Norwitz had just got married. She was working as a speech therapist at the Jewish Deaf Hostel and I warmed to her because she spoke so clearly and was easy to lipread, which meant communication between us was comfortable. I felt I could confide in her.

Valda and her family were good Orthodox Jews but led a secular life very different from my parents'. This made me realise that Jewish people could express their faith, lead simple lives and pursue successful professions at the same time.

She invited me to join her family to celebrate the beginning of the Sabbath on Friday evenings. How different it was from Friday evenings at home.

Valda encouragedv me to go out into the world. She felt strongly that I needed to broaden my perspective on life and develop my potential and self-confidence. I gradually became fascinated with the way she and her husband led their lives, and with their belief that Jews can contribute to the world and show God's glory through their work. A good education, successful professional career and moderate Jewish observance were their aims in life. Seeing that made me realise that I too could have a secular life without lessening my religious observances.

Valda was, is, and will always be a gem in my life.

CHAPTER EIGHT

A Difficult Year

A difficult year followed. When I was eighteen, my mother was involved in a very serious motor accident. One morning, as she was crossing a busy street at the traffic lights close to our apartment, she was knocked down by a speeding police car that was chasing another vehicle. I was at school at the time and my father, believing he was doing the right thing for me, tried to protect me from the truth about the ghastly injuries that she had suffered.

He rang Sister Thomasia, the Principal of my school, and explained that he did not want me upset, especially as it was the year of my matriculation exams. So all I was given was a message not to go home that night, but to go instead to the Jewish Deaf Hostel. He must have felt that they could look after me better than he could. That evening he brought my clothes to the hostel. He looked distraught but was unable to share his feelings or the details of the accident with me. All he would tell me was that my mother was in hospital, might be there for many months and that I would not be able to visit her there.

I was bewildered. I simply could not understand why I was being kept in the dark. I had no idea how serious things were or that my mother was lucky to be alive. I could only wait patiently over the next few months until my father felt able to confide in me, but even then communication between us was not easy. At last, six long months after the accident, he suggested I go with him to visit my mother in hospital.

Walking into the ward I looked at her in shock and disbelief. I was overwhelmed by what I saw. Her face was still bruised and her leg, still in plaster, hung in a stirrup above her. She was very emotional as she struggled to embrace me and I became most upset. I turned to my father for an explanation but he looked at me helplessly as if to say how sorry he was that he had not felt able to tell me before. I was filled with a sense of sorrow but in a strange way I had become resigned to the difficulties my father and my mother had always had, because of my deafness, in communicating with me.

A month or two later, my mother was discharged, her leg still in plaster, and I moved back home for my nineteenth birthday, although that turned out to be a very sad one. It was difficult for my mother to convey her needs to me. She would point at things she wanted and I would do my best to help. Slowly her leg began to heal and the plaster was taken off, but for a long while she was on crutches.

I was by now a young adult and able to express myself in sign language and old enough to make my own decisions. My parents could not always understand this and they seemed to believe that I still needed protecting. The details of my mother's accident were not the only important pieces of information that were withheld from me. Years later I would come to understand that others knew more about my eyesight than they were telling me.

However, now my father was beginning to realise what a mistake it had been to keep my mother's accident a secret from me. So when, very soon afterwards, my beloved Aunt May was diagnosed with liver cancer and was not expected to live long, my father did have the courage to tell me.

Aunt May, my mother's eldest sister, and Uncle Oscar, her youngest brother, had both had an unforgettable influence on my life. Because of my parents' difficulties with English, they had always helped in my upbringing.

In his bachelor days before he married his wife Dorothy, Uncle Oscar had lived with us and had been a wonderful example to me. He was a genuine gentleman. I never saw a hint of irritation or frustration in him. He was always calm and accepted whatever came to him in life. He was a major influence on me, and the compassion I learned from him was eventually to play an important role in my later life as a priest. It was his example that helped me to understand the important qualities of human life and gave me strength during that difficult year.

In her youth, Aunt May had left her home in Lithuania to be educated at a women's college in Brighton, England for a few years. After that, she had emigrated to South Africa where she married and started a family.

By nature May was such a loving person. She cared deeply for my mother and had helped her through all her difficulties in raising me, from my early childhood into my teens. She was a rock at the traumatic time of the diagnosis of my deafness and she helped my parents face the problem that so shattered their hopes. If it had not been for Aunt May, I think my parents would have raised me in a lifestyle like Tevye's, the main character in *Fiddler on the Roof.* Aunt May encouraged my parents to look beyond their own world and accept the secular environment around them and the outside support and education that I would need. Without her influence, I doubt that my parents would have even sent me to school.

As a small child, when they took me back to school on Sundays, I would get very upset and cry a lot. They found it very hard because of the lack of communication but Aunt May had always managed to calm me and soothe away my fears. She was such an encouraging person and she helped me accept boarding school.

I was always drawn to her beautiful smile. She, like my parents, had difficulties in communicating with me, but her kindness and her simple, powerful love were communication enough for me.

So now at nineteen when I learned that Aunt May was dying, I was devastated. My parents tried to discourage me from visiting her because they knew I would be upset. I think my mother had always been over-protective of me not just because of my deafness but because she had her own difficulties in dealing with emotions. So one day I went alone to see Aunt May in the nursing home, without my parents' knowledge. I arrived at her bedside and sat down quietly, without talking to her. In the silence I experienced a powerful and spiritual communication of love between the two of us. This was one of the most beautiful moments in my life and it gave me strength. She died very soon after and her death was to me more than just a simple separation. In fact, I feel a strong bond with my beloved Aunt May, even to this day.

Then came another severe blow. In June 1961, my father was diagnosed with cancer of the stomach. Despite the treatment he went downhill very fast and I remember so well the October when he paid his last visit to my school. It was as if he were checking up that all was well for me there. He confided in Sister Thomasia that it was his last fervent wish that I would do well in my matriculation, for that year I was to leave school and embark on my adult life as a young deaf man. My father knew that my educational qualifications would be the key to my future success.

As the exams approached I began to feel the strain. My mother could barely walk, my father was dying of cancer and I had lost my dear Aunt May.

On the afternoon of 7 November, I was called straight from my mathematics exam to the hospital and my dying father's bedside. My mother and I sat in an all-night vigil until, at four in the morning, he took his last breath and died peacefully. I remember walking home with my mother in the early morning light with such sadness in my heart. I asked her to ring Sister Thomasia and tell her that we had lost my father and that I would not be able to sit my last exam that morning.

Minutes later, Sister Thomasia rang back to advise me that it would not be a good idea to miss the exam. So I sat the English exam at nine o'clock that morning, with tears pouring down my cheeks as I struggled to keep a clear head amidst my grief.

Three months later I was rewarded with the news that I had passed my matriculation. Now I had to make my way in the world. What an unknown world it was to be.

I had no idea what career I should pursue, so again kind Valda came to my rescue. She took me to the University of Witwatersrand in Johannesburg where I took an IQ test and had a careers assessment. Three options were presented to me - social work, accountancy and engineering. Valda felt accountancy would have the best prospects and I did not argue, although I knew in my heart that I had leanings towards social work.

That would have to wait.

CHAPTER NINE

A New Faith Calls

Aunt Hilda, my mother's sister-in-law, and her husband Uncle Harry lived in England, but returned to South Africa every year. When I was young, she had been so concerned by my father's tales of the lack of Jewish education for deaf children in South Africa that she resolved to find out what was happening for Jewish deaf people in England. This led her to be a founder member of the Jewish Deaf Association in London in 1951, when I was nine. She was something of a pioneer.

When I reached the age of twenty-one, she thought that I needed to become more independent and she was keen for me to fulfil my potential. She felt I should not be so dependent on my mother and that I should learn how to handle money and look after myself. I had so much to learn.

Aunt Hilda encouraged me to venture out of the protected world of my family and so, despite my widowed mother's disapproval, I moved back to Berea and into a Jewish residential hotel. With nobody there to wake me up in the mornings, and wanting to be independent, I got myself my first piece of equipment for the deaf – a vibrating alarm clock to place under my pillow each night.

The Wyntonjoy Hotel was a renovated old apartment block that stood on top of a hill, looking out over the huge yellow spoil heaps of the gold mines. It accommodated sixty or more people of all ages, but mostly elderly. Some stayed permanently while others came for short stays or were booked in there by relatives who lived locally. It provided kosher food prepared strictly according to the rabbinical rules, or Beth Din, and followed all the Jewish observances.

My Uncle Harry and Aunt Hilda used to stay at the same hotel when they were back from England. Uncle Harry was a rather austere man, a good deal older than Aunt Hilda but still keeping himself active with his shipping company. I remember Aunt Hilda as a sophisticated lady, stylish with impeccable manners and with distinctly British tastes. She mixed with well-educated, highly cultured and wealthy people in both England and South Africa. She was very fond of me and I remember her teaching me to mind my manners and also how to pronounce words correctly so that I could be better understood by hearing people. She made a great effort to fill the gaps in my education where my parents had not been able to help.

At the same time as I moved into the hotel, I got a job as an accountancy clerk at the Greaterman Wholesale

Company, a few kilometres away on the eastern side of the city. I also started to study accountancy as a part-time student and I often used to go to the public library to do my homework. It was there that something of great significance happened to me.

I was doing my homework one afternoon, sitting at a large, varnished reading table. When I took a short break from my long hours of study, I sat back and looked around at the other people reading and studying. It was then that a large book on the table caught my attention. It was the *Summa Theologica* by Thomas Aquinas. I pulled it towards me and opened it. The section 'Life after Death' caught my eye and I began to read with interest. But when I reached the words 'Jesus Christ' I felt uncomfortable, closed the book and went back to my studies.

The next time I went to the library I found the same book on the same table which puzzled me until I noticed that the shelves behind me held all the volumes of the *Summa Theologica*. I ignored them and continued with my homework, but when I took a break, I found myself drawn to the book again. I turned to the chapter on the Resurrection, and it set me thinking about the Jewish and the Christian teachings on this topic. As I read slowly on, it struck me that the teachings in the Old and New Testaments had some similarities. I began to wonder what the differences really are between Judaism and Christianity. This was a question that continued to play on my mind and triggered in me some kind of search.

* * *

The hotel was built on a steep slope, and out of the small window in my basement room I had a panoramic view of Johannesburg, the 'City of Gold' that was founded in 1886 as a result of the Gold Rush. I could see the imposing building of the very modern Catholic Cathedral of Christ the King below, laid out in the shape of a cross with its massive walls and stained-glass windows. It had an elegant spire with a cross on top that looked as if it was made of gold and glinted in the sunlight. Sometimes I could see crowds of people filing up and down the steps of the cathedral on their way to or from services.

Every day, I would take the thirty-minute walk to work and back again to the hotel in the late afternoon. I enjoyed walking past the Great Synagogue, with its green copper dome and rusty Star of David on top of it. But, for some reason, at first I would not walk past the cathedral and took a detour to avoid it. After a while though, I changed my route, as I felt curiously drawn to the building that I could see from my hotel, but I still always crossed over to the other side of the road as I passed it. It was as if I did not dare to look at it too closely, and I often kept my eyes firmly fixed on my hotel, high up on the hill.

One beautiful, cool evening I was walking home enjoying the orange sunset. A soft wind blew against my face. Climbing slowly up the steep path I noticed something like a bright flash which at first I thought was a torch. It only lasted for a few seconds and was so strange and unnatural that I became quite frightened and almost held my breath as I quickened my pace. I hurried into the hotel lobby and headed straight for my small, dark room.

Later, in the dining room I felt safer, but I still had an underlying discomfort which I tried to hide as I took my seat beside Uncle Harry and Aunt Hilda who were staying there at the time. As usual, they nodded and said, 'Good evening, Cyril,' but I could see they had noticed my unusually pale face. Aunt Hilda asked me what was wrong, but although I wanted to confide in her, I resisted.

It was especially dark when I went to bed that night and then, in the middle of the night, I saw the same flashing light again just for a few seconds. It was really chilling and I broke into a cold sweat, not knowing what it meant. Drops of perspiration ran from my forehead and my pyjamas were soaked as if I had a high fever. I dived under the heavy woollen blanket but the flashing light started again. I sensed someone calling me: 'Come, follow me! Come, follow me!' I cried out loud. 'My God, God of Israel, help me!'

Immediately, the flashing stopped. I was completely exhausted and fell into a deep sleep. The next morning I woke up feeling very anxious, wondering what that strange sign had meant.

It was a late afternoon in January when, on the way home from work, I finally allowed myself to glance at the cathedral as I approached it. I even decided to stop for a short while - and then out of a compelling curiosity, I walked slowly to the big brass door. I opened it and peered inside. I saw the sunrays filtering through the stained-glass window on to a huge crucifix, which hung from a tall wooden canopy. Very tentatively, I went and sat down in a pew and gazed around this tranquil sanctuary.

Then fear crept into my heart. I thought, 'What is a good

Jew doing in a Catholic cathedral? Other Jews would think this complete blasphemy.' What was happening to me? Was I being invited to sit there quietly, in front of the altar?

After a few minutes I walked out of the cathedral and as I did so I realised that I had a growing fascination with the Catholic faith and that I needed to explore it. But the thought suddenly hit me that this exploration would lead me into an unbearable conflict with my love for the Jewish faith, and with my family. It was the beginning of a time of agonising uncertainty.

Shortly after this, I remade the acquaintance of an old friend from school who was eleven years my senior. Robert Simmons lived in an apartment block not far from my hotel and I used to meet him sometimes in the street. Like me, he was profoundly deaf, and until now, I had only known him by sight. I had seen him going into the cathedral and I wanted to get to know him better.

I immediately realised that Robert was an exceptionally intelligent man. He was at that time working in a medical research institute. Later he was to become a lecturer at the Medical School of the University of Witwatersrand in Johannesburg. I was also drawn to him because he too had been born into a Jewish family, although his parents were Progressive, rather than Orthodox Jews like mine. He had since converted to Catholicism. I had many deaf friends in the Jewish Deaf Social Club, but Robert was to become the first close friend who was not a practising Jew. We have been staunch friends ever since.

One day I asked Robert if I could accompany him to the Sunday Mass at the cathedral. He thought I was just curious and he had no idea that I was experiencing any inner conflict.

Inside the cathedral there was a fragrant scent of incense, as I looked nervously around at the people praying. Outside, the sun suddenly emerged from behind the clouds and its rays shone again through the stained-glass windows lighting up the crucifix on the altar. Suddenly, there and then, my heart recognised that I was being called. I had been in such a state of bewilderment ever since I saw the mysterious flashing lights and I knew that I had been searching for something very important. This was the sign I had been waiting for.

Going back up the hill after the Mass, Robert and I walked thoughtfully for a while. Then I turned to him and asked if the deaf people needed a priest. 'Yes,' he said, 'deaf people feel excluded and could only really be included if the priest could use sign language.' I was very pensive. Then, very nervously I asked, 'Do you think *I* could become a priest?' He looked startled and signed wildly, 'You must be mad! How can an Orthodox Jew like you become a Catholic priest? Your family would kill you.'

Red in the face, Robert looked as if he was going to explode. Gradually he became calmer, and said, 'Well, it is your own decision. But I must warn you, you may lose your wonderful Jewish family.' There was a long silence between us. Another journey was beginning.

CHAPTER TEN

Anguish

My conversion is such an abstract thing that it is difficult to describe my thoughts and feelings at the time. It was as difficult for *me* to understand as it was for my Jewish and Catholic friends and acquaintances, and of course for my Jewish family. In some ways it remains a mystery and it is still not easy to put into words the struggle I had as I moved towards what people saw as my new faith.

Looking back, I remember how my mind would go blank when people asked me about it and I could never explain it in terms of faith alone. To me it did not feel like choosing to give up one faith for another. It was not, as many people thought, that the love and care I had from the sisters at St Vincent's School had influenced me to give up Judaism. It is true that their warmth was something very important to me and that my parents, by contrast, had found it difficult to overcome the communication barriers. However, this was not the reason.

In fact, now I realise that the choice I struggled with, through the various phases of my conversion, was really not a choice at all. I have within me, even now, an acceptance of both faiths as equal, harmonious and complementary; something which maybe is beyond the comprehension and understanding of most Jews and Catholics.

Then, I was young and bewildered and mystified by what was happening to me. Robert's friendship was immediately very important to me. He suggested I should write a letter to Father David Walsh, a Redemptorist priest in the United States of America, who travelled extensively on preaching missions to deaf people in the USA, in South America and in Asia. Robert had met him in 1963 when he was at Gallaudet University and he suggested that I should share with him my desire for the priesthood. Later, Father Walsh was to advise me to come to Gallaudet University myself for a year or two to enable me to discern my vocation.

I had first heard about the university from a deaf school friend, and then later from Robert. He was sure that with the teaching that they provided specifically for deaf people, I could improve my English as well as broaden my knowledge generally, and at the same time work out my future. Some time later I did decide to apply for a foreign student's bursary, to save up money myself and to sell some of the Greaterman Wholesale Company shares that my uncle had previously suggested I buy. In this way I would be able to finance myself for two years as a student in America.

For now, though, Robert encouraged me to talk to my mother. This was when I really began to experience the pain of my conversion. Her response was agonising to me. 'My only child is giving me such unhappiness and causing me such shame in front of other Jewish people,' she said to me. I was speechless. I could not bear to be hurting her in this way and be shattering all her hopes in me. She asked me not to visit her any more because she felt so ashamed of me. In fact, she did not want to see my face again, she said. So resolutely did she set her mind on this that it was unbearable and I was plunged into darkness. Great sorrow and a long silence overcame me. I felt there was no one to offer me a solution except the God in whom I had trusted from my earliest days.

My mind turned to the good sisters of St Vincent's School, who I thought might lead me to an answer.

* * *

I knocked at the classroom door of Sister Fabiola. After Ralph Hahn had died she had been assigned to give us our Jewish religious education. She was very slender and very graceful. She had a great talent for storytelling. She acted out the stories, bringing them to life with such conviction that we were always spellbound. She was also a gifted teacher with a wonderful knowledge of the Old Testament.

Sister Fabiola opened the door. She saw my troubled expression and led me gently to sit down. With tears in my eyes, I told her that I wanted to adopt the Catholic faith. She listened attentively to my outpouring, but knowing how dutiful I had always been in my Jewish observances, she shook her head. She tried very firmly to dissuade me but I was insistent. 'How can God stop me in searching for my faith?' I asked her.

She softened a little. Then she suggested that she take me to see Mother Superior.

Mother Hildegretta, like Sister Fabiola, disapproved of the idea, and felt that my strongly Jewish upbringing would always predominate. I felt that they simply could not understand my inner voice and, over many weeks, I went on trying to convince them. Slowly they began to yield to my deep yearning.

Finally, Mother Hildegretta recommended that I visit Father Lloyd, the hearing chaplain for deaf people at the cathedral. So one afternoon I went to the cathedral and sat down in a side pew hoping to meet him. Almost immediately, he walked out of the massive door at the back of the sanctuary towards me. A short man with a fine head of brown hair and thick glasses, he headed straight to me and asked if I was Cyril. Astonished that he knew my name, I nodded and followed him into the presbytery. He explained that he had received a phone call from the school about my desire to embrace the Catholic faith and that he had agreed to give me catechism every week. I was overjoyed.

However, after a few weeks, Mrs Lurie, the matron at the Jewish Hostel for the Deaf, must have got to hear about it. She was a motherly lady and usually had a sweet smile, but she was so furious with me that she demanded to know the name and telephone number of the priest who was giving me the religious instruction. She also started to talk to others.

News of my new faith began to spread like wildfire within the Jewish community and friends and acquaintances started to ostracise me. Some were openly angry and critical; others were cold toward me or avoided me like the plague. At work, staff teased me and laughed about my new faith.

My nerves began to suffer. I could not sleep at night for my anguish and I felt despondent.

Then, one day, Father Lloyd called me to the cathedral. This lifted my spirits. I thought I was about to get the support I needed to cope with my difficulties. On the contrary, as we sat down together, I noticed his hands were trembling. He looked grave and very troubled, as he told me that he felt I should stop receiving his religious instruction. He pulled a letter out of his jacket pocket and handed it to me.

I unfolded it slowly and at once saw that the typed page was headed 'United Hebrew Federation of Synagogues'. It was from the Chief Rabbi. I realised immediately that Mrs Lurie must have told him. I read on:

> Cyril Axelrod, a born deaf person, has always been a fine example of a good Jew. His dedication to the faith has always been highly respected by the Jewish community. We appeal to Your Reverence, because we believe his conversion to the Catholic faith would be a great disaster for him and all of us. His late father insisted that a Jewish education should be provided for his only son. He brought the Jewish Hostel for the Deaf into existence. We firmly urge you to restrain Cyril from the religious education that would lead him to the Catholic faith.

My mind was suddenly in turmoil again. I felt moved to tears that Jews and Catholics were at that moment showing me their love and concern. Jews were attempting to bring me back to my community and Catholics were discouraging me from embracing their faith. What could I do?

Father Lloyd looked me straight in the eye. 'You cannot continue with your decision,' he said. 'You must go back to your own faith, Cyril.' I sat in silence, helplessly feeling that my journey could go no further. I stood up, thanked him and left.

I went straight back to the hotel and straight to my room in the basement. Darkness crept into my heart again. I could not eat for three days. Although I continued going to work, I felt so alone.

I did not give up. Something would not let the last small glimmer of light inside me go out.

After some weeks' reflection I decided to go and see Valda Norwitz. She was such an esteemed friend and although I did not want to hurt her feelings, I wanted to be utterly honest with her. I wanted to tell her that in exploring my faith I would have to go in a new direction and away from Judaism. She looked at me with incredulity. I could see that the news had shaken her badly; in fact that she was heartbroken. Again, I felt tense and weighed down by confusion. I was torn between my search for my new faith and my love and admiration for family and friends, especially the Norwitz family.

Seeing that I was unbearably confused, Valda quickly took control of her own emotions. She decided to take me to see a psychologist who might be able to help me. The psychologist worked with great sensitivity to explore what was happening to me but she knew nothing about deaf people and was a non-believer herself. In despair, I quickly realised that she would be of no help at all and that poor Valda's efforts had been in vain. My journey had to go on.

Then came the day that Aunt Hilda found out. I had been into the cathedral, still searching for an answer. As I came out, I looked up the hill towards my hotel. In the distance something caught my eye. To my horror, I recognised my aunt standing on the balcony. She disappeared as soon as I saw her but I realised I had been caught red-handed and that there was more serious trouble to face.

At supper that night, when I sat down with my aunt and uncle, she confronted me immediately. 'What were you doing in the cathedral, Cyril?' she asked me. I remained silent, not wishing to hurt her. I would have found it so difficult to explain. After we had finished the meal, she walked with me to my room and on the way said angrily, 'If you want be close to me, forget that place. If you continue going there, you will never see me again!' Her words shook me badly. I had always loved her dearly and admired her for the love she had shown to me and for her work with Jewish deaf people in England. I never wanted to hurt her feelings, just as I never wanted to hurt my mother's or Valda's.

Yet I still yearned to give my life to the service of God's love for deaf people. Ever since I had been told that I could not become a rabbi, I had felt a shroud around me. My desire to become a rabbi had never diminished but it was now what was leading me to want to become a priest. How else could I follow the vocation that God had for me?

A great sadness hung over my beloved Jewish family and friends, and other friends seemed afraid to help me. My churning thoughts and feelings weighed heavy on my young, frail shoulders. But still I would not let the small light in my heart go out.

So I decided to approach Father Gallagher, the Vicar General of the Diocese of Johannesburg. I told him of my desire to become a priest - but he looked at me doubtfully, saying it would be difficult for a deaf person to become a priest, and with little more discussion, he led me to the front door, politely giving me his departing blessing. I was stunned. I was being turned away, without so much as a hint of encouragement to study for the priesthood. Father Gallagher had only focused on my disability. My highest priority was serving God but it seemed that my deafness had stood in the way.

Valda continued to be so concerned about me that she tried everything to help me get through my state of 'confusion'. Without my prior knowledge, she and Mrs Lurie arranged a meeting for me with the retired Chief Rabbi, who had written the letter to Father Lloyd. He now lived in Israel but was on a visit to South Africa, and he agreed to come and meet me. I had no idea about this plan so I was happy to go with Valda on a visit one day to the hostel. As we went into the sitting room she broke the news to me that the Chief Rabbi was on his way to see me there. I was very shocked. I had a great respect for him and for his exemplary life and was extremely worried about what he would say or indeed what I could say to him. When he entered the room I began to tremble but his gentle manner made me feel a little easier. He told me that my attempts to go through a change of faith had shaken him badly. Almost in tears, I said, 'But God has a different plan for me.' He nearly wept himself, but nothing he said to me could make me change my mind. Soon he bade me farewell and went sadly away.

Valda comforted me that day, but she had finally come to the conclusion that I had to be left alone with my decision. I knew that splitting from Valda and my mother, and from my dear Uncle Oscar, in order to follow my faith, was going to be the hardest thing I had ever had to do, but we both knew that I must continue my unmapped journey alone.

CHAPTER ELEVEN

Vocation to Serve God

The difficult times continued. I loved my Jewish people but I knew I must leave them on my journey towards Catholicism. I was set on following my vocation to serve God through service to deaf people - but how?

When all else seemed to have failed, I suddenly recalled an incident long ago. Bishop Ernest Green of Port Elizabeth was visiting my school and came into the carpentry workshop. Confusing me with a fellow student, he asked me in fluent sign language if I was the boy who wanted to become a priest. Of course, at that time I wanted to be a rabbi and so I said, 'No, no, I am not a Catholic.' The teacher whispered in the bishop's ear and, embarrassed at his mistake, he apologised profusely. Then he turned to the other student and I saw his broad smile as he talked to him.

I realised now that, unlike the rabbi who had so discouraged me, Bishop Green must have been someone who would be willing to help a deaf person become a priest. I set my heart on meeting him again.

By now Bishop Green was well known for his forty years of missionary work with deaf people. As a priest in the Archdiocese of Cape Town he had established the Catholic hostel for deaf homeless people, just as Ralph Hahn had established a Jewish deaf hostel in Johannesburg. They had known each other well. Unexpectedly, Father Green had then been nominated as the Bishop of Port Elizabeth. At first he wanted to decline as the new post meant giving up the work with deaf people that he loved. However, the Vatican insisted and he was to carry on his ministry as bishop in Port Elizabeth for fifteen years.

I wrote to him straight away and told him of my desire to enter the priesthood. His response was immediate. He invited me down to Port Elizabeth to meet him in his chancery. I caught the next available flight and travelled the eight hundred miles south feeling excited.

In the morning I walked up to the main door of his cathedral. The secretary opened it and escorted me to the waiting room. The benevolent Bishop greeted me warmly. I reminded him of our meeting in the carpentry workshop at St Vincent's School all those years ago. He suddenly remembered me, and how he had mistaken me for the boy who wanted to be a priest. I laughed and he gave me a warm smile.

We discussed the need for a deaf priest to be working with deaf people. He told me he would positively encourage

81

such an appointment. Then he asked me directly if I would be interested in becoming that priest. I nodded. He beamed with delight, saying how much it would mean to him to see me as a deaf person ordained as a priest. There and then he put the application form on the table and began to fill it out for me. He needed to know the names of my parents and their faiths. 'Your father must have been a Catholic?' he asked. I shook my head and told him he was a Jew. The Bishop smiled but went on to say, 'Oh, so your mother is the Catholic?' Again I shook my head. 'She is a Jewess,' I said. He raised his eyebrows. 'What about you?' he went on. I grinned. 'I shall be baptised very soon.' He nearly fell off his chair in astonishment. 'You are not a Catholic yet, but you wish to become a priest?'

At that, Bishop Green handed me a book of Simple Catechism but I told him I had already read it. 'I am reading the *Summa Theologica* of St Thomas Aquinas at the moment.' 'Well, Cyril,' he said, patting me on the back, 'First of all you need to be baptised, then come back to me and we'll talk about the priesthood.' He led me to the door, and said as I left, 'Cyril, I shall pray for you.'

Three months later I was baptised in the chapel of St Vincent's School for the Deaf. It was 14 August 1965. I was twenty-three years old. I had always been a good Jewish boy, and here I was, without my family there, being baptised into the Catholic Church. It seemed unthinkable. With my dear friend Robert Simmons as my new Catholic godfather, I took my vows. Also there, were the sisters whom I had known throughout my schooldays, and a small group of my close friends. The young chaplain, Father Sean Murphy, who had earlier been so worried about my decision to embrace a new faith, performed the ceremony. That day held such significance and joy for me.

The following day was the Feast of the Assumption of Mary, one of the most important feasts of the Catholic Church. At the Eucharist, I walked up to the altar in the Chapel at St Vincent's school with my new godfather by my side. The elderly priest, Father Ramsey, brought the Holy Communion to me and I received the Body and Blood of Jesus for the first time. As he handed me the blessed bread and goblet of blessed wine, it struck me immediately how similar this was to our Jewish Friday nights. I thought of my good father saying the Kiddush over the bread and wine. Amidst the joyous celebration of my reception into the Catholic Church, I had a moment of deep sadness as I thought of my Jewish family and friends, who could have no part in it.

To me, there seemed to be so many similarities in the two faiths and my conversion to Christianity from Judaism did not feel as radical as some people thought it was. It did not feel like a painful departure from a tradition of faith I had grown in and loved all my life. The pain arose only from the misunderstanding and even rejection by those close to me in the Jewish community. I did not see my conversion as a 'departure' so much as a continuation into a new experience and a full flowering of my Judaic faith. I believe that Christianity, centred as it is on Jesus Christ who is son of David, son of Abraham and thus a true child of Israel, is the offspring of Judaism. My conversion was based on a spiritual progression and not on a separation. I think that the first

Jewish converts to Christianity would have experienced something similar. The Council of Jerusalem in the first century of Christianity marks the realisation in faith that God chooses not only the Jewish people but that His love flows in abundance for all the peoples of the earth. Rooted in the experience of God's relationship with my Jewish ancestors, I found myself blossoming in the 'catholic' knowledge that God's love knows no boundaries but is universal.

CHAPTER TWELVE

My Seminary Years

The two years at Gallaudet University were like a watershed in my life. They prepared me in so many ways for four more years training - for the priesthood – when I returned to South Africa. With Gallaudet's tailor-made teaching for the deaf, my English grammar improved and my intellectual horizons broadened. Mixing with other deaf students, with whom there were no communication barriers once I had mastered American Sign Language, I became more confident and independent as an adult deaf man. I also spent time studying philosophy at the Catholic University of America which was in Washington DC as well, and so I was able to discern my future.

By contrast, back at the St John Vianney Seminary in Pretoria, the four years were to be long and hard. At times I felt that I was marooned alone on a desert island. Being a deaf man in a hearing seminary, often not knowing what was going on around me and unable to lipread lectures, was a painful and frustrating experience. I did not know then, though, that years later, I would be enrolling on a course of study, not only as a deaf man but also as a blind man.

From the very first day at the seminary I knew it would not be easy. I arrived there accompanied by my former teacher Sister Vincent. A seminarian introduced himself to me and offered to carry my baggage. He led me off across the garden towards my room, talking as we went. Then it dawned on him that there was something amiss. I was not responding to him. He turned round to see why, and smiling at him, I said, 'I cannot hear! I am deaf.' He was so taken aback that he dropped my baggage on the garden path and hurried away, leaving me alone. Another seminarian ran to me offering his help. He too was clearly nervous of me as he led me down the corridor to my sparsely furnished room and he too quickly disappeared.

As the days went by, I was aware how difficult the other seminarians found it having a deaf man in their midst. Many were afraid to approach me and whenever I walked along the corridor, it seemed to me that other students would flee when they saw me. Bishop Green must have heard about this because early one morning, dressed in his black cassock and purple cincture and looking very concerned, he popped into my room to see me. 'I know how you must feel, living in a place like this. But it's only for a short time. Persevere for the priesthood, Cyril.' After he had gone I sat on my bed for a while, thinking that, until now, I had had no idea what it meant to be deaf in a hearing world without support. From then on, I kept remembering Bishop Green's advice: 'Persevere for the priesthood.' The faith he placed in my ability to succeed touched me greatly.

In lectures I sat in the front row, trying hard to lipread the professors, but it was impossible. They kept walking up and down, turning to face the blackboard and moving their heads from side to side. I asked the student next to me to take notes for me, giving him a sheet of paper with a piece of carbon paper underneath it. He agreed reluctantly but I became alarmed when after the first forty minutes he had not written a thing. 'Don't worry,' he said, 'The professors should provide the notes for us.' I was dismayed. I could not afford to waste so much time sitting in the lecture halls while the professors' words flew past my ears and eyes.

The next day I plucked up enough courage to go and see Father Norbert, the Father Rector of the seminary, a man of great monastic spirituality and compassion. With tears in my eyes, I tried to explain my difficulties. I pleaded to be allowed to study in my room instead of going to the lectures but Father Norbert said that it would not be possible. I implored him, 'How is a profoundly deaf person supposed to *hear* the lectures?' At that point he was moved to kindness and said he would talk to the professors.

The following day, Father Norbert called me back into his office. My request to study in my room had been approved on a six-month trial basis, provided that I took some tests in the lecture room from time to time. He recommended that I visit each professor to get his notes. My room became filled with the huge pile of papers and books that they gave me, and it became my own personal sanctuary from morning to evening. I had to work really hard to understand the theology and it was quite a struggle to keep myself alert and focused on my studies. Remembering Bishop Green's words though, I plodded on.

After the six-month trial was over I sat my first exams and won Father Norbert's complete confidence in my independent method of study. It was almost unheard of in the seminary for a student to study alone, but he said I could continue to work in my room for the remaining three and a half years of the course. Gradually some of the students became friendlier and I slowly began to be able to integrate more and more with them.

On one occasion, I asked a seminarian to help me make a phone call in the telephone booth that was tucked between our dining room and the corridor. He promised he would be back in a few minutes to help. While I stood waiting for him I became interested in the instructions on how to make a call. Following the directions I picked up the handset as if to dial a number. I suddenly became aware of an audience behind me. I spun round and demanded, 'What's the matter? 'A miracle, a miracle!' cried one of them. 'You can use the phone! You can hear!' I burst into laughter and explained that I was just following the instructions out of idle curiosity while I waited for help.

Another incident that amused me happened one afternoon. After lunch the seminarians would usually gather together in the chapel and recite from the Divine Office, the daily prayer book for Catholic priests and religious, composed mainly of the Psalms. Once, while this was going on there was a loud explosion in the vicinity of the swimming pool where a build-up of water pressure had forced the lid off a huge water tank. All the other students rushed outside to witness the chaotic scene. Water gushed from the tank and flooded the pool and its surrounds while they ran to turn off the stopcock. Blissfully unaware, I continued reading the Office. When the students returned to the chapel to finish their reading, puzzled, I asked if something had happened. When they told me, I leapt up to see for myself. Then we all burst out laughing at my delayed response and excitement.

In my second year, I was inducted to the status of a cleric, with a formal liturgical ceremony making me a sub-deacon. Sister Thomasia, my old school Principal, had had her quiet confidence in me rewarded. She had kept in close contact with me during my difficult time at the seminary and even organised for me the support of Mrs. Goddard, a warm-hearted Jewish lady who was a voluntary speech therapist.

Sister Thomasia's continued belief in what deaf people could achieve was inspiring. Determined to share this, she rang my mother to ask if she would like to attend the ceremony. My mother had mixed feelings as she had not seen me for a long time and at first politely refused. Thirty minutes later she phoned back to tell Sister Thomasia that she had changed her mind, but I did not know this. Later, Sister Thomasia asked me whether I thought my mother would come. I shook my head sadly and she told me not to be too disheartened.

The day of the ceremony arrived. Sister Thomasia, the Mother Superior, accompanied by Sister Aquilina and several of my old teachers, came to the seminary. Sister Thomasia told me to go outside to a car where someone was waiting for me. Imagine what an overwhelming and emotional moment it was for me when, as I stepped out of the seminary door, I saw my mother for the first time in three years.

I greeted her warmly and escorted her to the front row of the chapel. She was nervous and uncertain. She had never been in a chapel and she later told me it felt more like a cinema! I hurried to the sacristy to tell Bishop Green of my mother's arrival. He was already in his vestment and mitre, but he took them off to go and embrace my mother. This incident touched the hearts of all who were there.

The ceremony began with the bishop placing the white surplice on me. The celebration of the Eucharist followed. My mother, more relaxed now, sat quietly, smiling at the seminarians and professors around her, but not really understanding what was happening.

After the ceremony, my mother was invited to join the tea party. Father Norbert, chatted with her, making her feel at home with what to her were 'foreigners' or 'goyim'. During their conversation she told him of her sadness as a good Jewess that she had no one to celebrate the Sabbath with on Friday nights. She wished that her son could read the prayer to honour the Sabbath with her but he had abandoned his Jewish faith forever. She left the seminary without saying another word to me, leaving me quite uncertain as to whether she had accepted my new faith or not.

The next day Father Norbert called me to his office. I was anxious because I remembered how Father Lloyd had turned me away from embracing my new faith for the sake of my mother. This meeting was different. The Rector was very reassuring. He asked me what it would be like for me to pray with my mother. I told him that I would do anything to respect her and to please her. He smiled, and to my amazement and delight he encouraged me to celebrate the Friday Sabbath with her. With that he reached inside his brown Franciscan habit and handed me his car keys, saying, 'You can go home every Friday to celebrate the Kiddush with your mother and come back after the Sabbath.' I was filled with joy that the Jewish faith still had a place in my life.

I arranged to drive home the very next Friday. After three years the house still looked just as beautiful. My mother had prepared the table with the silverware and crystal glasses. The covered Challah bread lay between the two silver candlesticks that were my grandmother's and I could smell the familiar aroma of kosher chicken broth wafting from the kitchen. I felt nostalgic. Tears came to my eyes as I recalled those days when I celebrated the Sabbath with both my parents.

This time my mother had placed the leather-bound Hebrew prayer book, inscribed with the golden Star of David, at the head of the table, and my black velvet skullcap on top of it. She embraced me with the Jewish greeting: 'My son, you are blessed with the Kiddush in the dining room.'

My mother sat opposite me at the table. We covered our heads, mine with the skullcap and hers with a laced scarf. She lit the candles and stretched her hands over them, praying softly. Then she gave me a nod. I opened the Hebrew prayer book and recited the Kiddush slowly, just as my

91

father had done, blessing the wine and the bread. It was the first time I felt a real 'Jewishness' after a long period of 'excommunication'. After the blessing we ate the traditional chopped herring, beaming with happiness. My mother then brought out the consecutive courses of delicious kosher dishes.

It was a deeply moving reconciliation, as together we honoured God and His Sabbath. What a special experience it was for us both – a Jewish mother and her Catholic son!

Our 'Friday nights' continued throughout the rest of my years at the seminary. After I had been home a few times for the Sabbath, my mother presented me with a generous gift – an Austin Mini car. This enabled me to travel easily to her house each week. Father Norbert had shown extraordinary compassion and understanding for my mother, and her desire to have me celebrate Jewish observances with her. He was delighted by our reconciliation and I will always be deeply grateful to him for bringing it about.

During the Passover and the Jewish New Year celebrations my mother invited some of the other seminarians to join us. The Catholic students were intrigued by the novel experience of being fed by a Jewish mother. At the same time they developed their own theological understanding of Jewish celebrations.

On one occasion, I went shopping with my mother for kosher food the day before Passover. She wanted to buy a leg of kosher lamb but they had sold out. She could not possibly contemplate a Passover meal without lamb. I saw that there was lamb for sale on the opposite counter. 'Mother, let's buy that,' I said. She refused adamantly, saying, 'It's not kosher!' Using my wits I replied, 'Mother, as the descendant of Aaron, the High Priest, I will pray to God to make it clean and change it to kosher.' She was amused. 'You can't do that. Only a rabbi can.' 'Well, I am a *Catholic* rabbi!' My mother, although not completely convinced, accepted my advice. At the Passover meal, she tentatively tested a piece of the meat. 'It tastes just as nice as kosher lamb,' she said. I smiled at her. 'That is because it has been blessed by the Lord,' I said, with a mischievous twinkle in my eye. I was so happy that our communication was much easier now that I was used to being with hearing people.

It was a pleasure to be able to share moments like that with my mother after all we had been through. I was well aware of my future of celibacy and that I would never be able to get married, or become a parent myself or share such a moment with my own child. It was a sadness to me for I greatly value the institution of marriage and the family.

As a younger man I had two or three girlfriends, all of them deaf, but my mother had always counselled me not to marry a deaf girl when I grew up because she feared that we would have disabled children. When I was twenty she invited a hearing Jewish girl to the house in the hope that she might be a good match for me. My mother, who seemed to believe that I could not speak for myself, spent the entire evening talking to her. I resolved that that would be the last time I allowed my mother to try to find me a romantic partner!

* * *

93

I often wonder how different things might have been if I had been born hearing and not deaf? Some people have asked me whether I would have become a rabbi, which would have left me free to marry. I think the answer is no. I think it is more likely that had I been able to hear I would have been drawn into my mother's family business, working with my uncles and remaining in Johannesburg for life.

Being born deaf broadened my horizons. I did have an interest in business and I certainly enjoyed my early accountancy work but it was not enough for me. It did not give me the opportunity to make the contribution I wanted to make to others. I had seen the suffering of deaf people – the lack of learning and the lack of opportunities for self-expression and autonomy - and I wanted to share with them what I had learned. I wanted to make a difference to people's lives.

It was then that I knew that marriage was not going to be for me, for I knew I would not have time for a wife or for conventional family life. So my commitment had been made long before I had to start preparing for my vows of celibacy.

However, soon after the kosher lamb incident, my godfather Robert and his wife May did give me an opportunity to experience something of the parental role.

After obtaining his doctorate, Robert had decided to take a well-earned week's vacation with May after the many years of working on his thesis. He asked me to look after his four young children: Vivienne, aged two; Alex, three; Paul, six; and David, who was eight.

I trembled with anxiety. I realised I had no idea how I

would cope with and properly care for these four playful, mischievous and highly-intelligent, deaf children for a whole week. Would I have the ability to be a competent carer? I turned to Father Norbert for his advice. To my surprise, he thought it was a good idea, suggesting that it would be an invaluable opportunity to experience genuine family life.

As I drove along the highway to Johannesburg, I thought about what it might mean to act as both a father and a mother at the same time to these children. Should I be tender or strict? So many questions went through my mind but I reminded myself that if I was going to become a priest, I needed to trust in God, so I resigned myself to His will.

When I arrived at the elegant house, the front door quickly swung open. Four children peered out and one signed to me, 'Are you here to entertain us?' I was by now very nervous and could hardly raise a smile. Robert and May sensed my anxiety and quickly reassured me of their complete confidence in my natural ability to look after their children.

As soon as their parents left the house, the four children with their new-found 'freedom' became over-excited and charged uncontrollably about in the garden. My heart pounded as I attempted to calm their wild antics but they took little notice. Never before had they been like this with me. As an only child myself, I had no experience to draw on of sibling behaviour. I had to learn very quickly.

I was at my wits' end when I caught sight of Vivienne crawling along a high wall in the garden. I could not imagine how she had climbed up there. 'Come down, my dear,' I cried as I frantically waved my arms. She looked down at me, but just grinned and waved back. I ran to get a chair to fetch her down. When she was safely on the ground I firmly reprimanded her and, to my astonishment, she immediately calmed down. From then on, I was more or less back in control of the children. Although it was only for a week, the challenges and joys of being with four young children gave me some insight into the role of parenthood.

The more I learned, the more I appreciated my experience of living with the Simmons children. It helped me to see the importance of family life in God's love. This brief glimpse would benefit me enormously in my counselling work later and allow me to empathise with deaf people who were bringing up children. I owe the Simmons and their lively brood a debt of gratitude for that.

They also helped me to see how different it can be growing up in a deaf family. The Simmons family shared a common language – sign language – so communication was free-and-easy and natural. Events of the day, jokes, sadnesses and joys could be shared together as in any family. The children absorbed an understanding of the world around them just like any other children; they developed abstract ideas and concepts and shared their natural curiosity and learning with their parents without any impediment. How very different from my own experience growing up with hearing parents and in a family where feelings could not be expressed easily. I could never tell *my* parents what I had done or learned at school.

Nevertheless, I am grateful that I did have access to speech, lipreading *and* sign language. In my later work in the Far East particularly, I would find that sign language interpreters were few and far between, and that my ability to lipread and make myself understood using my voice would be invaluable in my negotiations with the hearing authorities and government officials, and in learning other languages.

CHAPTER THIRTEEN

Ordination

My theological studies were complete. The date for my ordination to the priesthood was set as 28 November 1970. The ceremony was to take place at the Cathedral of Christ the King, Johannesburg, the same cathedral that I had held in such awe all those years before.

At the time, my mother was taking a long vacation in Cape Town with her brother, Oscar, but I hoped that she would be able to attend the ceremony. It seemed that that was not to be. Uncle Oscar persuaded her to stay away, and so three days before my ordination she sent a telegram to tell me she would not come. My heart sank. It was such a shame that her family had influenced her and tried to separate us in this way. I was sad and disappointed and so were my friends and colleagues who had looked forward to meeting her, but I resigned myself to God's will.

Then on the very day before the ordination another telegram arrived. Against all family pressure, she had changed her mind and decided that she would come to my ordination after all. How delighted and happy I was.

The Sisters of Mercy organised accommodation for her in a small cottage near the convent. To make her feel at home, they stocked the fridge with kosher food and removed all the religious pictures from the wall. When my mother arrived at the cottage, she did not stop to look at the rooms, but went straight to the refrigerator. She beamed, 'This place looks so wonderful. Just like a Jewish home.'

Next day the cathedral was packed. There were deaf people from all over South Africa and deaf children from St Vincent's School. There were Dominican sisters in their black veils and white habits, and members of the parish. Both side chapels were filled with priests from all over the Diocese of Johannesburg and further afield. Father David Walsh and Father Tom Berst came as representatives of the International Catholic Deaf Association, and two bishops – Archbishop Garner of Pretoria and Bishop Boyle of Johannesburg – sat in the sanctuary.

My mother and two Jewish friends – Mrs Claude Goddard, the voluntary speech therapist, and her mother Mrs Marks – joined my close friends sitting in the front pew. Behind them sat the Sisters, the deaf children and my other deaf and hearing friends.

The Master of Ceremonies and altar servers led the procession with over thirty priests, Bishop Green and myself. The procession began at the presbytery, moved along the street and through the main door of the cathedral while pupils from the Rosebank Convent sang hymns from the choir loft.

Bishop Green took his place in front of the altar facing the congregation and was flanked by the gentle Father Frank Doyle, who had taught me classics and Church history, and Father David Walsh, a committed supporter of deaf people and a member of the Redemptorist order. Three different sign languages were used simultaneously throughout the ceremony. My godfather, Dr Robert Simmons, translated into South African Sign Language, Father Walsh interpreted into American Sign Language and Bishop Green used Irish Sign Language.

I was led to the front pew and sat between my mother and Mrs Goddard (two Jewish mothers!). When Father Frank Doyle called out, 'Let those to be ordained to the priesthood come forward,' the two Jewish mothers immediately stood up with me and, holding my arms, led me to the Bishop. He greeted them warmly, asking, 'Do you wish to offer your son to the altar?' Smiling, my mother and Claude Goddard replied, 'Certainly,' and each turned to give me a kiss.

It touched the hearts of all who witnessed it, my Jewish mother offering her only son to the Catholic Church. It was a very moving ceremony and brought people to tears. Then, making it even more moving, the Bishop read the story of Hannah and Samuel (1Samuel1:1-28). Hannah, like my mother, offered her only son to the Temple in gratitude for her gift from God.

During the traditional hymn of invocation to the Holy Spirit, the Bishop knelt before the altar while I prostrated myself face down on the marble floor as a sign of my total commitment to God as a priest. It was a deeply moving experience for me as I gave up my spirit and body to my God in heaven. After that, the bishops and priests in turn placed their hands on my head, invoking the Holy Spirit.

The Bishop had made the whole ceremony more accessible for the deaf congregation by allowing me to face them. He questioned me on my willingness to obey the pope, my local bishop, and the priestly ministry. I pronounced in Sign three times 'I do.' The Bishop invited the deaf people to come to the sanctuary to gather around him and me. Mrs Goddard placed on me the priestly stole and vestment, which had been made by the Dominican sisters. As she did so, I suddenly remembered my Bar Mitzvah all those years before, when my father so proudly placed the brand new prayer shawl on my shoulders. The Bishop anointed my hands with the sacred oil of chrism, special olive oil blessed for ordination, as a sign of my new priestly office, spreading it all over my palms. It was a means of visibly indicating to deaf people that I was anointed to the priestly life.

He then took the beautiful gold paten and a chalice carved with an image of the Risen Christ and the word 'Alleluia' and placed them in my hands. At that moment, kneeling before the Bishop, I remembered my dear father handing me the goblet of red wine and the Challah bread shortly after my Bar Mitzvah, inviting me to say the Kiddush for the first time. My mother's heart had swelled with pride and my father gently nodded his approval. It had been such an important occasion for them to have their son recite in Hebrew this special prayer on a Friday night for the first time.

The chalice that the Bishop now gave me had an inscription on the bottom, 'Presented to Father Cyril Axelrod on the occasion of his priesthood on 28 November 1970, by all the deaf friends of South Africa.' As he handed it to me with the paten he said, 'Accept this offering when you offer it as the sacrifice for your people.' He then led me to the altar to exchange the sign of peace with the bishops, the priests and the deacons.

I then joined him, as the main celebrant, in offering the Sacrifice of the Mass for the first time. It was the culmination of Aaron's sacrifice in the Old Testament. At that moment, my dream of many years ago to become a rabbi was in a way fulfilled. The long journey from disappointment was over. The priesthood had become my new goal. God had opened the door for my new journey of hope and faith.

After distributing Holy Communion, the Bishop brought me to the altar and invited me to bless him. Then I proceeded to the front pew where my mother and Claude Goddard sat together. I put my hands upon my mother's head and bestowed the Jewish blessing on her in Hebrew, 'Hear, O Israel. The Lord God is One. May the face of our Lord, God of Abraham, Isaac and Jacob, shine upon you.' I then did the same for Mrs Goddard in English. My heart swelled with pride and happiness as my dream to bless my mother as a 'rabbi' was fulfilled. It was also the realisation of many years of hope to be able to minister to deaf people, irrespective of their faith.

At the conclusion of the ceremony, which had been so unusual, I gave the blessing to the people as the beginning of my ministry. It was a moment of the most joyous celebration for my mother, my Jewish friends and all the people who witnessed it.

The celebrations were not over. The following day I celebrated my first Mass as an ordained priest at the Church of the Immaculate Conception in my home parish of Rosebank. It is sometimes called the 'blue church' because the interior is painted sky blue and it has beautiful blue stained-glass windows. What a wonderful atmosphere was created when the sun shone through the glass spreading its gracious blue rays!

I celebrated the Eucharist – the breaking of the bread and drinking of the wine – for the first time as the priest. Seven priests were there, including the Redemptorist Vice-Provincial Superior at the time, Father Anthony Pathe, and so was my mother. Again the church was packed from the Communion rail to the back pews with parishioners and deaf friends, and the Sisters from St Vincent's School.

After the Mass, the priests joined the congregation in welcoming my mother. They all smiled and applauded the Jewish mother and her son, as if we were like Hannah and Samuel in the Temple. I was so happy but my mother's feelings must have been quite mixed. She had for the first time witnessed her son participating in the Catholic liturgy and now was experiencing the warmth and support of the Catholic people, but she was after all a strict Jewess.

17. First year students at St John Vianney Seminary, Pretoria, 1967. I am kneeling.

18. The congregation at my Ordination to the Priesthood in the Cathedral of Christ the King, Johannesburg. 28 November 1970.

19. Deaf pupils of St Vincent's School for the Deaf and Sisters at my Ordination to the Priesthood.

20. My mother leading me to be ordained.

21. My Ordination by the Right Reverend Ernest A. Green, then Bishop of Port Elizabeth.

22. Giving my first blessing at the Ordination – the Jewish blessing to my mother.

23. At the end of my Ordination with Bishop Green.

24. Giving Holy Communion.

25. My first Mass as an ordained priest, at the Church of the Immaculate Conception in my home parish of Rosebank, Johannesburg. 29 November 1970.

26. With my mother and Bishop Green the day after my Ordination.

27. The photograph of me as a newly ordained priest that hung on my mother's wall.

CHAPTER FOURTEEN

My First Work
with Deaf People

After the joyful celebrations of my ordination there were to be new challenges for me. Now at last I could begin my ministry with deaf people. Only two weeks after I had become a priest, however, I heard news that shook me badly. Bishop Green had resigned his office and was to return to his former ministry among deaf people in Cape Town. Without him as my bishop I was uncertain as to what the future might hold. He had been instrumental in my becoming a priest and I was afraid that continuing my journey alone would be like returning to that long, dark tunnel.

The day before Bishop Green resigned, he assigned me as chaplain to a school for Black deaf children in a rural area near King William's Town, a small city in the Eastern Cape Province. This was to dash the hopes of the deaf community in Johannesburg who wanted me as their priest. They were angry because they felt that I had been taken away from them for no good reason. I knew God must have His reason.

Most of the schools for deaf children in South Africa had been set up by Catholic missions and of course then were operating strictly within the government's apartheid policy. St Thomas' School for the Deaf where I was sent was no exception. It was one of the schools that an Irishman, Father Donal Cashman, had set up. He was now the parish priest.

The school and its buildings were in a forest. It was very remote. There was no radio there and no newspapers. The telephone was the only means of keeping in touch with the outside world. Of course, I was unable to use a phone and did not get my first text phone for deaf people until a few years later.

The school was run by four Dominican sisters and some dedicated teachers. The three hundred deaf pupils were all Xhosa people. Under the apartheid policy the Government insisted that African languages be used, and so teaching at the school was in their mother tongue, the Xhosa language. I soon discovered that Xhosa uses tongue clicks as part of the language and I set to work at once to learn enough to communicate with the children and teachers, both in Xhosa and in their tribal sign language.

The apartheid policy meant that all the pupils were Black and were not allowed to make contact with deaf people from other ethnic groups in South Africa.

The biggest shock for me was to discover how isolated

115

the deaf children were from their parents who mostly lived on farms far away. The children were only allowed home for holidays twice a year, and usually had little or no communication with their families. So after a few years they regarded the school as their home and often did not want to leave at the end of their elementary education as they had little chance of building careers at home. The apartheid policy certainly destroyed family life by forcing deaf children to be separated from their families. It created a communication barrier between parents and children, which meant that the deaf children kept in closer contact with their own deaf peers with whom they *could* communicate.

I stayed in the mission for three years. It was hard for me because I lost contact with deaf people in the cities. Some of them begged me to come back to develop pastoral work among the deaf community in Johannesburg and I dearly wanted to do that. I was also worried about my mother living there all alone. Her heart had sunk when I moved away and she was sad that I could not say the Kiddush with her on Friday nights, although Father Cashman was sympathetic and encouraged me to travel the seven hundred miles to Johannesburg occasionally to keep in touch with her.

In June 1971, I was also given the opportunity to leave the school for a few months to go on my first preaching mission abroad.

First of all I went to schools for the deaf in Rome, Florence and Bologna. The Piccola Mission Congregation, which runs the schools, had several deaf sisters and brothers. The highlight of my stay in Rome was a private audience with Pope Paul VI. I was led to the main gate of the

Apostolic Palace by Father Vincenzo Blais. With him was Dr Irealla who was deaf himself and had been a founder member and first President of the World Federation of the Deaf. From there, the Swiss Guards wearing their orange and blue uniforms and large, dark blue berets with small red feathers, escorted us to the Palace.

We walked through a room that had magnificent frescoes by Raphael. More Swiss Guards stood in the corridor wearing silver breastplates and Spanish metal helmets with maroon feathers. We were then brought to the antechamber, whose walls were made of Italian marble. The gentleman-in-waiting, wearing a tight silk jacket with ruffled shirt and black trousers, gave us instruction on how we were to greet the Pope. We were expected to kiss his ring.

We waited a while for our turn to enter into the audience room. It was a simple white marble room with a small throne on a dais, the papal coat of arms hanging above. On the throne sat a frail, aged, but smiling Pope, wearing a white cassock and skullcap.

The Pope greeted us warmly. The gentleman-in-waiting introduced each one of us to him. When we attempted to kiss his ring, he humbly and gently pulled back his hand and shook his head. Upon hearing my name, a beaming smile crept across his face. He beckoned me closer and asked, 'Which diocese do you come from?' 'Port Elizabeth, South Africa,' I replied shyly. 'Ah! Bishop Green informed me that he had ordained you. You are the first deaf priest that I have met!' As he embraced me with warm congratulations, he asked me to convey a message to my mother. He said he admired her as a Jewess, presenting her only child to God,

117

and wished to thank her for her gift to the Church. He blessed me and said, 'Go out to preach the love of God to deaf people.' The Pope's kind, firm words moved me to tears. What wonders God had performed for me.

As I was escorted out of the Apostolic Palace I took one last look back at the Pope. The meeting became one of my most cherished memories. I was able to follow the Pope's instructions, travelling around the world on preaching missions to the deaf from 1971 onwards.

My next stop was Paris, to attend the Congress of the World Federation of the Deaf. Deaf people gathered to discuss education, psychology, spiritual care and other activities. I was amazed to find so many deaf people from all over the world actively participating in service to their own communities. That strengthened my confidence in my own priesthood and my own service to deaf people. It seemed that God was using me for something more than I had expected. My mission was to be to lift up the hearts of deaf people and empower them with the hope and expectation that they could serve the Church themselves and that the Church would strengthen them.

In Paris I also had the wonderful experience of meeting Father Burnier from São Paulo, Brazil. He was the first deaf priest in the world, while I was the third. I met him again in Geneva to discuss the issue of pastoral workers for deaf people. There, I had another chance to meet pastoral workers from Churches of different denominations, stretching from Syria to America, from Africa to Europe. Although we followed different doctrines through God, we shared a common love for deaf people.

Also in July 1971, I was the only South African delegate attending the first International Catholic Conference on Education for the Deaf in Dublin. Priests and sisters from all over the world came together to discuss religious education. A small group of active religious teachers from England and Ireland were also present. I was fortunate enough to be able to get to know the Irish and the British deaf people there because I had learned both their national sign languages in South Africa. Afterwards, following the Pope's instruction, I travelled without a break from one Irish town to another preaching to deaf people before returning to South Africa.

A year before I left St Thomas' School, the administrator who was in charge of the Diocese of Port Elizabeth, in the absence of a bishop since Bishop Green left, thought it would be best for me to work back in Johannesburg. He could see the needs of its large deaf population and that it would be good for me to keep in much closer contact with my mother. Eventually, after another year, I was seconded to the Diocese of Johannesburg to begin my pastoral work there.

CHAPTER FIFTEEN

The Redemptorists

It was when I was back working in Johannesburg that I had my full introduction to the Redemptorist order. Founded in the eighteenth century near Naples, by St Alphonsus Liguori, this group of missionaries remains faithful to this day to his vision. They dedicate their work to the poorest and most abandoned in society. Today there are nearly six thousand Redemptorists working in seventy-six countries around the world, helped by many men and women who support their mission.

I knew a little about the order from my travels in the USA. A fellow student at the seminary in Pretoria had also once taken me to a service at the nearby Redemptorist church. It was a novena service held weekly for devotional prayer to Our Lady of Perpetual Help.

Later, Father Stephen Naidoo, himself a Redemptorist who was to become Archbishop of Cape Town, came to Johannesburg to run courses of spiritual renewal for the sisters. I used to go to see him from time to time for spiritual guidance myself. He noticed that I was feeling lonely and was finding it difficult to keep up with my spiritual exercises. 'You are a community person, Cyril. You should not be living alone in your ministry.' I did not grasp what he meant at the time.

Part of my work involved driving up to a school for the deaf in Hammanskraal every week. This was a long and frustrating journey. Father Stephen suggested I should break my journey and spend one night a week at the Redemptorist Monastery in Pretoria. I jumped at the idea.

The Monastery was a two-storey square building, painted white and with a tall bell tower. It had a vaulted cloister that added a great air of contemplative serenity. I rang the front door bell and was greeted by a lean young theology student, who turned out to be Larry Kaufmann. Straight away his amiable and reassuring manner put me at ease, for I had been a little anxious He showed me up to my room which had a real monastic feel to it - spacious but with only a bed, a desk and a chair in it. Larry told me the times of community prayer and meals and then left me alone.

Later, I went down to meet the other confrères, priests and students. They were all wearing their black Redemptorist habits, but despite their strict monastic dress, they were sitting in comfortable armchairs relaxing and chatting in the common room. It was not at all what I had expected.

I already knew that Redemptorists, although living an

121

austere way of life, were not an enclosed contemplative order. The Redemptorists that I was meeting now were active missionaries who went out from their monastery to preach throughout Pretoria and elsewhere in South Africa. Nevertheless, I expected them to be serious, formal and very solemn at all times. I was wrong.

When I went into the room, one of the confrères, Father Joe Duffy, announced, 'Here comes Cyril. He is someone who really knows what it is live in a community.' I did not fully understand what he meant but I was introduced to and greeted each one of them. I recognised one of the students, Michael Fish, who used to be involved with the Christian Life Group at my old school. He had attended my first Mass and it was particularly good to see him again. The warm welcome I received from everyone at the monastery was deeply heartening and much appreciated.

My weekly visits there gave me a great feeling of strength and renewed my energy for the long trip to the mission station in Hammanskraal. At this stage though, I was still firmly attached to the secular life of a diocesan priest and had no thoughts of a monastic or community life.

Then one day I was in the common room. Because of my deafness I was not fully involved in the conversation and so decided to retire to my room. Larry Kaufmann saw me go. He sensed that I might be feeling isolated and followed me, just to keep me company. I was touched by this friendly gesture. Afterwards, I asked myself, 'Is this what you are searching for, Cyril - a community life and spiritual companionship?'

Tentatively, I expressed my growing desire to lead a

community life to Father Naidoo. He smiled. 'I have been waiting for you to say that.' He knew that I needed to live in a community. After all, I had been used to the school community, the deaf community and the Jewish community. I was really quite a community person.

However, for some months I was torn between wanting to join the Redemptorists and my attachment to my dear mother. When I mentioned this to her she shook her head despondently and said, 'My son is going to leave me for good.' I tried to reassure her that that would not happen but her reaction had added to my doubts. I did not want to hurt her more than I already had. I discussed my dilemma again with Father Stephen and he assured me that God would take care of it. So in May 1974 he wrote a letter to the Vice-Provincial Superior of the Redemptorist order in South Africa asking him to allow me to join.

I soon received his reply that I was welcome and Bishop John Murphy of Port Elizabeth, who had succeeded Bishop Green, also gave me his blessing. The year for which I would be a novice in the order would start the next January. I was most excited at the prospect, and any reservations I may have had I left to God.

Meanwhile, the Rector of The Monastery in Pretoria invited me to dine with the community on 1 August, which was the feast of St Alphonsus, founder of the order. They shared my joy that I was going to join them and we had drinks before lunch to celebrate. At one o' clock, Father James McCauley answered a telephone call from Johannesburg, and immediately called me away to my room. He gently broke the news to me that my mother had passed away that morning. It was such a shock, as the day before we had been out shopping together and she had seemed fine. I had offered her a lift home but she wanted to carry on shopping. That was the last time I saw her, my lovely Jewish mother.

* * *

Speaking to God through my tears, I sobbed, 'O dear mother, you gave me as your only child to God.' Michael Fish came to comfort me, and said, 'St Alphonsus is taking your mother's place. He will look after you.' I took great solace from this. I felt that it was part of God's wonderful plan to place me in the care of the Redemptorists at that time and so lift from me my anxieties about my mother. And he did it on the very day that was the Feast of St Alphonsus.

I also remembered that a few months earlier my mother had spoken with courage about when her time would come. 'Although I have felt so hurt for a long time, I am happy for you, Cyril, that you have found your new faith, but I want you to respect my wish to die as a Jewess and be buried in the Jewish cemetery.' I had struggled to hide my tears and said without hesitation, 'Of course, Mother.' She also asked me to pray for her once a year wearing my prayer shawl (*talith*) and my phylacteries, the two small boxes with leather straps containing the Ten Commandments. One phylactery is placed on the forehead and the other near the heart with the strap wrapped around the left arm seven times and on the left hand in the shape of *shin*, standing for *Shema*, which is the profession of the One True God. Even now, I still do this once every year in memory of my parents.

124

Three days later, my mother's funeral took place in the Jewish cemetery in West Park, Johannesburg. A small group of Jewish relatives and friends were there and so were several of my Catholic friends, priests and students, some of them Redemptorists.

It was a full Jewish funeral. As is the custom we met in the Omen, the special square room at the cemetery, where we waited for my mother's coffin to be carried in and placed in the centre of the room. It was a simple Jewish coffin, plain and unvarnished, covered with a black cloth with nothing but an embroidered Star of David on it, and no flowers at all. As the closest relatives, Uncle Oscar and I stood in front of the coffin and the Cantor cut off our shirt pockets to mark the beginning of eleven months' mourning. Prayers were said and then folding doors opened along one side of the room that would lead us out into the cemetery. The Cantor read out the names of those male relatives chosen to guide my mother's coffin on its trolley to her burial, close to my father's headstone. After fifty metres or so, more prayers were said and then, because there were so few relatives there, he called for volunteers to take a turn in guiding the coffin for a further fifty metres. I felt wonderfully supported by the Redemptorist priests and students when eight of them stepped forward to help and I think my mother would have been pleased too. Finally, at the graveside, after the coffin had been lowered, Uncle Oscar and I recited the Kaddish, the Jewish prayer of mourning, for my dear mother. Later, a headstone would be unveiled, facing north to Israel, just as the Talmud dictates.

It was all just as she would have wished, but with her

death I felt sure that I would never see my Jewish family again. With a heavy heart, I resigned myself to this as I said 'good bye' to them after the funeral that day.

CHAPTER SIXTEEN

Identity and Faith

My mother's unexpected death was a great blow to me. It was more than a simple separation between us. During my five years' priestly life, her presence had somehow provided me with a link between my identity and my new faith. She had always kept me aware of the richness of my Jewishness and always spent time on the preparations for each Jewish festival, encouraging me to celebrate them with her. She was determined to keep me involved in her practical faith and I really valued that. It meant that my new faith could grow in harmony with my Jewishness. It was my mother's dear hope that I would be able to find a way of integrating identity and faith in my life.

With her sudden death, I felt that integration dissolve. Thinking that there would never be another person like my mother, who could give me such a special gift, I felt as if a door had closed and that I was at the end of a journey. I thought that my contact with Jewish people had come to an end.

I never for one moment imagined that my older cousin, Claire Baecher, whose cheerful and forgiving nature I had always valued, might slowly come back into my life and in a way step into my mother's shoes and provide an anchor for my Jewishness.

It was an excellent surprise a few weeks later when she made a phone call to the cathedral and invited me to come to her house for the Sabbath dinner on Friday. It was as if the door was opening again. Nevertheless, I hesitated to accept the invitation because my mother had told me that no one else in the Jewish family could accept that I had changed my faith and become a Catholic priest. Claire, however, must have been aware that my hesitation was a sign of my inner struggle and she did not give up. She phoned again and asked me to come the next Friday night.

I drove to her house. I was wondering what her attitude toward me would be, and I resolved to be cautious, and not let myself get too close to her. I was delighted when the door was opened and Claire gave me the warmest of welcomes. There was not a trace of ill feeling. She led me to their balcony and introduced me for the first time to her husband Rudi who had originally come to South Africa from Czechoslovakia. Despite their friendliness, I was still reserved, but not for long.

Claire sat down beside me and opened her heart. 'We are close cousins, Cyril. I know our parents were not close to each other but let's forget the past and look forward to our renewed relationship.' My caution melted away. She went on, 'Cyril, you are most welcome here at any time. Come and celebrate the Sabbath with us whenever you can. I will give you a key to the house so that you can come and go as you please.'

Unlike my mother, Claire was not an Orthodox Jew but observances like Friday night were important to her. She was, and still is, a woman of remarkable family spirit and reconciliation. Her outgoing personality and her empathy gave me tremendous consolation at that time. Like my mother, she could see how important it was for me to find a way of integrating my Jewish identity with my new faith. She gave me great encouragement and became like a warm ray of sunshine in my life. I know that my mother would have been overjoyed.

Not long after, Claire's loving-kindness for me was echoed by that of another cousin, Dawn Raphaely, who also encouraged me to try to integrate my identity and my faith. Just before the Jewish New Year she invited me to spend a few days with her family. The next day her gentle husband, Steven, took me to the synagogue for the prayer service. I was worried that my presence might not be welcome there but Dawn had encouraged me to go. Sitting in the front pew Steven gave me a prayer shawl and the prayer book both in Hebrew and English. I felt my heart swell with happiness and pride that I was being granted the honour of participating in the thanksgiving for the Jewish New Year once more.

The next day was Sunday and in the morning Dawn drove me to the church to say Mass for the Black deaf community. It was another example of her wholehearted support and understanding of my Jewish identity and of my Catholic faith. The door that Claire had opened for me, Dawn opened a little wider.

* * *

My trip to Israel later that year was another landmark for me. I was now a Catholic priest but this visit to the land of Abraham was very important to me. I thought I might be open to criticism, but when I landed on the soil of my fore-fathers I felt a great sense of belonging to the people of Israel, and our history stretching back for centuries. I could see around me a Jewish identity that I could share but here it was blended together within a multitude of cultures and languages that had been brought there by so many Jewish immigrants from their homelands.

In Jerusalem, the oldest city of Israel, I saw the three faiths coexisting - Jewish, Christian and Muslim - and this had the most powerful impact on me, encouraging me to reconcile and unite my own inner identity and faith.

By the Jaffa Gate rabbis and Jewish worshippers passed by saluting me, '*Shabbat shalom*,' and I returned the cordial greeting while priests called to me, 'Peace be with you.'

At the Western Wall, often called the Wailing Wall, a young man put a prayer shawl on my shoulders and phylac-teries on my arms and forehead inviting me to join the other Jews as they faced the wall in continuous prayer. I was delighted. It gave me a wonderful opportunity to reflect upon my parents and my family and my Jewishness but at the same time reaffirm the Covenant with God in my prayers.

One day I climbed Mount Sinai reaching the summit at sunset. There, again I was overwhelmed by history as I stood where Moses received the Ten Commandments. I thought of Moses asking God who He was and receiving the simple answer, 'I AM WHO I AM.' The scene thereafter came to represent to me a symbolic seal affirming the close relationship between Moses and the God of Abraham, and affirming also the Covenant between God and myself. It was a powerful experience and I trembled with emotion.

Just before Christmas I was invited to celebrate Chanukkah, the festival of lights, at the home of Jewish friends in Tel Aviv, and then only a few days later I went to Bethlehem to celebrate the Christian festival of Christmas in the Church of the Nativity. This too reinforced the sense of integration for me. It seemed that there in Israel, touched by the many historical and religious influences, my soul had found the seal of unity between my Jewish identity and my Catholic faith. My mother, Claire and Dawn and my visit to Israel had made that possible.

I did not know then that some years later I would return to the Western Wall with three other Redemptorist priests. This time I would bring my own skullcap, prayer shawl and phylacteries with me and I would put them on over my black shirt with the Roman collar. A Jewish gentleman would ask me quizzically if I was a Catholic priest, and I would smile at him and say, 'No, I am a Catholic rabbi.'

CHAPTER SEVENTEEN

The Novitiate

Back in South Africa, a month before I was to move to Cape Town for my novitiate, the Redemptorist Novice Master wrote me a letter. He explained that I was to bring only one suitcase and only a few clothes and to have a cleanly shaven face. Rather grudgingly, I had to accept that the beard I had had for more than ten years, which made me look rather like a rabbi, must come off. It was the start of a new life. The novitiate programme was to be the transition for me from individual to community life. For so many years I had been looking for that - a life in which family and community take precedence over the individual, like the Jewish culture I had grown up with.

I arrived in Cape Town and Bishop Green took me to The Monastery. It stood next to the Holy Redeemer Church

132

and had panoramic views of Table Mountain. I stood in the monastic gardens with Bishop Green and felt the tranquillity and peace of the place, as the sun sank down. I thought to myself, 'This is going to be the perfect place for prayer and meditation.'

The Novice Master was an elderly man, with a slight hearing loss himself, who originally came from Scotland. His manner reminded me at first of an army sergeant. He took me on a tour of the buildings. The linen room was painted a bright pink and I could not help commenting on what a horrible colour it was. 'Is God giving me a test?' I asked. His face remained impassive. I realised he did not share my sense of humour.

Later on, I also realised that he could not comprehend my profound deafness. He used to complain, 'Cyril never listens when I call him.' Once, when it was time for our manual labour, I was asked to put dead leaves in a wheelbarrow and throw them into the fire. I was pushing the wheelbarrow along the path and he called out my name behind me. He did not seem to realise why I did not respond until a young novice whispered in his ear that I was deaf.

Despite this, though, and despite his stern manner, I soon realised that the Novice Master had a heart of gold. One afternoon, one of my chores was to wash and clean the outside of all the large windows in the Monastery. It was such heavy work using cloths and window rollers that I had the idea of using a hosepipe instead. As I was doing it he came up behind me and tapped me on the shoulder. It gave me such a fright that, as I spun round to see what he was saying, the hosepipe pointed straight at him. For a moment

I thought I might be dismissed from the order for my 'mischievous' behaviour but his stern look suddenly dissolved and he saw the funny side of it as he danced from side to side, trying to avoid getting his black habit wet.

The Novice Master was not the only person who misunderstood my deafness at first. I had communication difficulties with my confrères too. They did not seem to be aware of my need to lipread or to use sign language and I was beginning to expect a very tough life ahead in the community.

In fact, I began to doubt that I had the perseverance needed to become a Redemptorist. I went to see the Novice Master about the possibility of leaving the order. He sat at the desk opposite, looking pensively at me. He was silent, which made me feel very uncomfortable, but then he spoke. 'You came here when your mother died to experience community life. You have your difficulties with communication but you can still do it. We are all here to support you.' With this encouragement, and thinking of my mother, I resolved to take up the challenge. My commitment to become a Redemptorist was re-affirmed and my first year was completed with the customary ceremony of the profession of religious vows of poverty, chastity and obedience. It was the next step in my journey.

I now had to leave The Monastery in Cape Town and return to Pretoria where I was assigned to live with the community of Redemptorists for three years to prove that I could fit into their way of life. At the same time I was to continue my pastoral work with deaf people. These three years were to be my 'temporary' profession as a Redemptorist, after which I would make my 'final' profession.

28. Old pupils at St Vincent's School for the Deaf after my Ordination, 1970.

29. Staff from St Thomas' School for the Deaf, near King William's Town, Eastern Cape Province, visiting St Vincent's School for the Deaf, Johannesburg, after my Ordination. 1970.

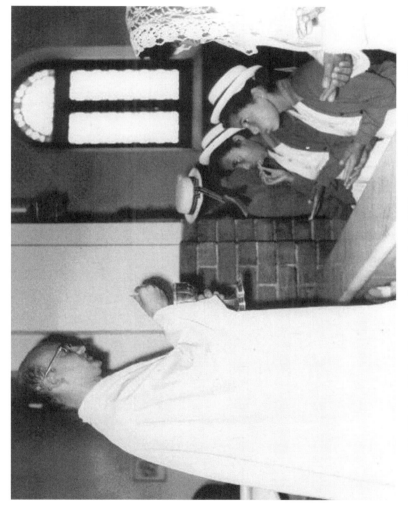

30. Giving Holy Communion to deaf children in Cape Town, 1971.

31. My mother's grave in Johannesburg Jewish Cemetery, 1974.

32. At The Western Wall, Jerusalem, 1978. I am second from the right.

33. My skullcaps, prayer shawl and phylacteries.

CHAPTER EIGHTEEN

The Challenges Begin

For the next seven years I was to work both in Johannesburg and Pretoria. My mission was to set up various projects and develop services for deaf people in different places, regardless of their race or creed. I was even able to maintain my links with Jewish deaf people and offer ministry to them as well. It was also a time when I travelled widely outside the region into different parts of Africa and beyond, on short preaching missions to deaf people.

From the first day at The Monastery in Pretoria, Father Kevin Dowling, who was the Vice-Provincial Superior of the order in South Africa at this stage, gave me considerable encouragement. Always supportive, he believed that human abilities and values are more important in community life than any difficulties or limitations that disability or deafness could bring. He said to me, 'Your life's mission is not only to go out and serve deaf people but your disabilities are also your mission to the Redemptorists. Your presence here in The Monastery will benefit all your confrères as they learn from your disabilities about human limitations.'

I did sometimes run into difficulties there because of my deafness, but some of my confrères learned a little sign language and how to fingerspell, and Father Dowling's confidence in my contribution never diminished. He gave me responsibilities just like the other hearing confrères and he never thought that my work would be hampered by my deafness. In fact, he liberated me from that disability.

I started work straight away. I grew back my 'rabbi's' beard. My first task was to develop a service for the unemployed deaf people in Johannesburg. That is when Sister Mannes, recently retired from forty years' work in a school for the deaf in Cape Town, and now living in a convent outside Johannesburg, became my devoted personal assistant.

I set up my office in a high-rise building in central Johannesburg and she worked as my secretary, answering the phone and writing letters. With her dedicated support, I focused on my pastoral ministry but also on supporting the social and human development of the deaf community.

My mission took me into Soweto, just outside Johannesburg. I was shocked by the conditions of poverty and poor housing that the Black people in that township had to endure during apartheid. There were often five to ten people in one room with an outside toilet shared by two families. There was no money for food, clothes or education.

I felt ashamed because I had had such a good life and a good education. I could not bear to see how they lived and it made me resolve to try to improve the situation for deaf people there through my work.

In June 1976 hundreds of Soweto high-school students gathered in protest against inferior Black education and specifically against being forced to speak Afrikaans in school. The police responded with tear gas and then with gunfire. Three people died and a dozen were injured. The angry Soweto residents reacted by burning government buildings. More police and troops with more guns were sent in. Hundreds were killed and the troubles continued well into the next year. I did my very best to support deaf Black people through these terrible times.

One evening, I had just finished giving a service for deaf people who had come to church to pray for those who had been killed. It was very dark and we only had candles for light. I could see lots of car headlights coming towards the church, and I said to the people, 'Please go home. Go home quickly,' because I could see it was the police. Twelve police cars came and surrounded the church. When I went outside four White policemen came up to me and asked me what I was doing. I told them I was giving a service, a memorial service, for the Black people who had died. They snatched my prayer book from me and made as if to arrest me. I was very scared. It was very difficult for me but, thank goodness, I found the courage to say I was only doing my job giving a service to Black deaf people and I would continue my work whatever. Luckily they only gave me a warning.

One day in 1978, I was called to visit some deaf patients

at the Baragwanath Hospital in Soweto. While I was there, I called in to see the speech therapist. I found her in a small, crowded room where a group of fifteen Black deaf children were sitting waiting for their therapy. Every day their parents dropped them off early in the morning before going to work, but after a lesson of only thirty minutes there was nothing to do all day but wait to be picked up again in the evening. There were no vacancies for them in any schools for the deaf.

Deeply shocked and very upset, I went to see the head teacher of St Martin's School in Soweto to ask if a spare room could be found for these children. Sister Leah understood my concerns but told me that the school already had two thousand children in it and another thousand on the waiting list. I felt appalled at how deprived these Black deaf children were, with no chance of schooling and no chance of any opportunity later on in life. The fact that they could not even get on the waiting list made their future seem hopeless. I was close to tears but she must have been touched by my pleas and by my voice, for she said, 'That is how *you* learned to speak so well, is it?' She went on to reassure me that something must be done.

A few months later she phoned to say that she had managed to free up a storeroom. All that we needed now was the finance. Some weeks passed and then a large envelope arrived at my office from Rome. It contained a cheque for sixty thousand rands, worth then about twenty-five thousand US dollars, or twenty thousand pounds sterling. I was overwhelmed by God's providence.

On 1 October that year, forty deaf children, aged two to

fifteen, moved into their new premises, which now had desks, chairs, a teacher's table and a blackboard. A retired teacher of the deaf agreed to teach them and later they swapped the storeroom for a large classroom that could be divided into two for the younger and older children.

The children came from different ethnic groups in Soweto, making it impossible to decide which language should be used. The Special Education Department for Black Disabled Children insisted that the Zulu language be used, which provoked a storm of protest from some parents. I pleaded with the government to allow English to be used in schools for Black deaf students so that they could have a language in common. I was persistent until eventually they gave their permission. In this way, the school became the first day school for Black children in South Africa using the English language - a historic landmark in this country under the rule of apartheid. This little classroom in North Soweto was later to become the much bigger Zizwile School, and it eventually grew into a large educational and technical complex with over five hundred deaf students.

Meanwhile I continued to travel every Friday to Hammanskraal to the mission station for deaf children, where I gave Mass and religious education in Setswana Sign Language. On Sundays I paid home visits to White deaf people in Johannesburg. I said Mass in a mixture of British and South African Sign Language at St Vincent's School for the Deaf and in Irish Sign Language for deaf people who had come from Cape Town.

I travelled widely to remote villages in Zimbabwe, Mozambique, Swaziland and Lesotho. I would find one deaf person and send him word that I was coming. When I arrived, there would be a large gathering of Black deaf people and I would say Mass in sign language and give what pastoral and moral support I could. I also ministered to Jewish deaf people in Johannesburg. My association with them before and after my conversion had remained a solid rock of friendship and loyalty. Although I was a Catholic priest, Jewish deaf people still regarded me as their 'rabbi', for they did not have one of their own. I was invited into Jewish homes to discuss the meaning of the Talmud and Jewish festivals. The fact that they could not worship at a synagogue upset me greatly.

Although I was aware of the difficult relationship I had had with the Great Synagogue, I attempted to arrange a meeting with the rabbi there but sadly nothing came of it. Some years later my cousin Claire's stepdaughter, Alice, did arrange a meeting with the rabbi at the Progressive Jewish Temple. Expecting him to ask, out of curiosity, about my priesthood, I was somewhat nervous. However, he received me kindly, listening attentively and sympathetically as I explained to him the great need for spiritual care among the Jewish deaf community. Although he was uncertain, Alice and I managed to persuade him. He finally asked her to develop a programme for a special sign language interpreted service on Fridays so that deaf people could be included. It was a dream come true for the Jewish deaf people and over sixty of them assembled for the first accessible service since Ralph Hahn's death.

The service was the highlight of the year - deaf people returning as 'lost lambs' to participate in worship at the

Temple. The rabbi told the congregation that deaf and hearing people were equal in the worship of God. He also said that this was surely the first time that a Catholic priest had made worship possible for Jewish deaf people. I was most grateful to him for making it happen and glad that they should feel included in the Jewish community. I was only sad that, because of a preaching mission I was conducting in Durban, I could not be there myself.

Later, however, I learned that the interpreter had not been experienced enough and that deaf people had struggled to understand her. The deaf attendance slowly tailed off, and to this day Jewish deaf people in Johannesburg still do not benefit from any spiritual care, although a few deaf people persist in attending worship without ever truly understanding what is happening.

It has always been my hope that one day Jewish deaf people all over the world will be able to enjoy the privileges of Jewish observance just like their hearing counterparts.

CHAPTER NINETEEN

Breaking Down Barriers

The second phase of my pastoral work started after my 'final profession' ceremony in 1979 when I had completed my three years in the Monastery and was now fully accepted into the Redemptorist order. Claire and her husband Rudi and Dawn and her mother René, my Jewish cousins, had attended the service. It was a beautiful occasion, with Claire doing the first reading - about Abraham leaving for the Promised Land.

The main project in this phase of my work was to build a hostel for Black deaf people in Hammanskraal just outside the city of Pretoria. Set in barren land, Hammanskraal had a few shops owned by Black businesspeople that stood slightly set back from the main road. The people living in sprawling rows of shacks behind them travelled daily to work in

Pretoria. They would get up at half-past four in the morning to be bussed to the city and return home late at night. Although you could reach the city from Hammanskraal by car on the main road in forty minutes, the buses collecting the villagers from different rural communities took two hours to reach the city. The apartheid policy meant people from those areas were limited by 'influx control'. They had to produce passbooks to get into the city and many were in this way denied the possibility of earning a living.

The hostel was designed to accommodate Black deaf people coming from distant farms to work in the city. Archbishop Daniel of Pretoria made it possible by finding the site between the Dominican school for the deaf and the St Paul Minor Seminary. As chairman of the project, he entrusted me with the finance and building of the hostel.

We called it Bobokweng Hostel for the Deaf, *bobokweng* in Setswana meaning 'place of progress'. It consisted of five rooms each housing four residents, two classrooms, a dining room, a recreational room and also a caretaker's room, which I eventually moved into when my office in Johannesburg closed down.

Bishop Green officially opened the hostel in 1979 in the presence of government representatives, my cousins and friends. There were also Church personnel (priests and sisters), members of the deaf community, and many support-ers and benefactors.

One government representative remarked that it is like the Covenant made to Abraham. 'The deaf people are leav-ing their homes to improve their quality of life. The Covenant marks a challenge for the deaf people to recognise

149

their lives as the gift of God.' Some years later due to the inconvenience for the workers of travelling between the hostel and the city, it moved to Mabopane, about fifteen kilometres from of Pretoria, where it remains to this day.

Both in Soweto and Hammanskraal, and later when I began the third phase of my work in Cape Town, I learned a great deal about oppression and injustice. The apartheid policies isolated, marginalised and humiliated the Black people and the so-called 'Coloureds' who were of mixed race. The policies prevented deaf people from different ethnic groups from meeting together or sharing a common language. The social and political oppression systematically removed from deaf people any chance for human learning, for gaining knowledge or information or wisdom. It left them with anxiety, frustration, a feeling of worthlessness and above all, crippling poverty and the constant threat of eviction from their 'sub-economic' homes.

Their plight and poverty affected me deeply and I resolved that my mission must be to build bridges of communication, to stand for solidarity with them, to build morale and confidence, to help them find ways of keeping their homes and maintaining the importance of family life, and strengthening deaf communities. Most of all I wanted to encourage deaf people use their intelligence and talents and build their own self-worth as valuable human beings.

Sister Mannes had moved from Johannesburg to a convent near the Hammanskraal hostel to continue as my assistant. One day she handed me a letter from the USA that filled us both with disbelief. I had been nominated for the Edward Miner Gallaudet Award. Dr Edward Miner

150

Gallaudet was the founder of my old university, and the award is still the highest award for deaf people. It was a great honour for me to fly out to Washington DC to receive it, inscribed with the words 'Serving the deaf people in their human values and needs in the International world'.

Two years later it was an equally great surprise to be selected as one of the recipients of the South African State President Excelsior Award for outstanding service to people with disabilities in South Africa. Because of my mixed feelings and those of my community, I sought guidance from Archbishop Denis Hurley. Although he was an outspoken critic of the government, he encouraged me to take the award on behalf of disabled people. I attended the lavish ceremony and was presented with my award by President Botha. The huge audience of Afrikaners rose to their feet to sing their national anthem in Afrikaans - such a contrast to the Black deaf people that I served whose human rights were being denied by the apartheid regime.

Throughout my work in Africa, I knew that because of my comfortable upbringing and my education, I could never know the suffering and poverty myself, but it was wonderful that gradually, during the long years of the injustice of apartheid, Black deaf people began to share their feelings of pain with me as I worked alongside them in their struggle.

As well as the pastoral support I could give, I was eventually able, with the permission and blessing of my Redemptorist community, to give some financial assistance out of my dear parents' inheritance. Also, in the years following, I asked several large companies to sponsor some

151

deaf people for higher education and career training.

With this support several deaf people went on to make great achievements both in and outside South Africa. Among them are a Member of Parliament, a qualified teacher, a special assistant to the President of a university, a highly qualified computer technician and the manager of an academic computer-training unit. What made me feel so pleased was that they were able to achieve what I had achieved. Moreover, they still carry on the philosophy of empowering deaf people and serving their own deaf communities.

For example, when, in 1987 I was assigned to a ministry with deaf people in Cape Town, I worked with the Rev. Nicholas Bruce, a Catholic deacon, and a deaf social worker Wilma Newhoudt, to set up a new organisation, Deaf Community of Cape Town. It was unique, and thought to be revolutionary, in that it was the first multi-racial association for deaf people under apartheid, enabling all races, White, Black, Coloureds and Indian to socialise and to work together in one deaf community.

When my ministry called me to the Far East, Wilma and the Reverend Bruce carried on the work. Later his deaf wife Susan and other deaf people set up a sewing project at the Deaf Community of Cape Town Centre, to offer employment opportunities. Wilma later graduated from Gallaudet University and she was still there in 1994 when she was invited back to South Africa for a special occasion. By then I was in Macau but I was invited back to join her at the opening of a new and expanded Social Centre in an ex-army barracks in the affluent Cape Town suburb of Newlands. To

152

our surprise a plaque dedicated to both of us, as co-founders of the Deaf Community of Cape Town, was unveiled. To this day the community is entirely run by deaf people.

My eighteen years of service in South Africa showed me the real suffering of deaf people, the poverty, deprivation, injustice and inequality. In my pastoral work I have not only tried to share with deaf people the richness of faith but also the richness and importance of human self-worth. It is my belief that learning, information, knowledge and wisdom are gifts from God. Whatever the social or political situation, whatever the disability, these are the gifts that liberate us from any form of oppression, fear or anxiety. There is always a way of fulfilling one's life using God's gifts and the deaf people of South Africa have shown this through their wonderful achievements.

CHAPTER TWENTY

Retinitis Pigmentosa

I was not prepared for what happened in 1980.

Still living in Hammanskraal, I set out for a three-month preaching mission in the USA, visiting twenty-seven of the fifty-one states. While in Nebraska, staying at the Redemptorist House in Omaha, I tripped and fell down a long flight of stairs. I had not seen the step properly and also when I looked up I noticed something that looked like curtains on both sides of the large window, although I knew there were none there. I was mystified and felt an immediate surge of anxiety.

I was apprehensive as I flew the next day for an appointment with an ophthalmologist at Kansas University Medical School. The Professor's diagnosis was shattering. He told me that I had retinitis pigmentosa (RP), a progressive disease of the retina, which would make me blind within five years.

In the days that followed I headed off to Washington DC to see my confrère and good friend, Larry Kaufmann, who was now studying theology at the Catholic University of America. Walking together one day, and with a large lump in my throat, I told him my news. He was speechless but I told him, 'God has already used my deafness to serve my people. Now he will use my blindness.' Larry was as supportive as ever.

Later, I went for a very thorough second opinion at the Massachusetts Eye Clinic in Boston. The retinal specialist who examined me asked me lots of questions about my family's medical history but the one question that seemed to confirm his diagnosis was, 'How old were you when you learned to walk?' 'Three,' I replied, slightly unsure how that could be related to my eyesight. With that he smiled and said that it gave him the answer he needed to complete his diagnosis. 'Father Cyril,' he said gently, 'You have Usher syndrome. It is a condition in which you are born deaf and then later go on to develop retinitis pigmentosa. Late walking and poor balance can be some of the symptoms. Your retinas are gradually breaking down.' He explained that first my night vision and then my peripheral vision had been affected and that in time I would develop tunnel vision, which over the following ten to twenty years might lead to blindness.

With that, memories suddenly came flooding back, and in the days and weeks that followed I went over and over in my mind all my past experiences that could have been caused by this eye condition.

155

When I was ten years old, my parents took me on a long railway journey to Cape Town. The train had a long stop at Kimberley, where I got off to stretch my legs. On the platform, I accidentally collided with the huge, bulging stomach of a very portly stationmaster. He was furious. With a fiery red face and popping eyes, he grabbed me and shook me vigorously. My father who had witnessed this, rushed to my rescue. He told the stationmaster that I was blind. This instantly made him let go and quelled his fury. Instead, he admonished my father, telling him to be more careful with me. When we were safely back in our compartment, I asked my father why he had said I was blind. He did not reply.

At school my coordination was poor and I was very clumsy, which irritated other children. I remember bumping into them when we rolled tyres in the playground. I also remember being reprimanded for not joining in with sports. I would rather sit alone watching and be told off than miss the ball or get in other pupils' way on the playing field. Once, I hid in the toilets but was soon found and received the cane for my disobedience. I tried to tell my father about it but he did not seem to understand. I became rather withdrawn and something of a loner, and although I was studious and did well at school, teachers would sometimes say that I was not paying attention properly. Children often poked and prodded me to get my notice. Was any of this to do with my eyesight? Was that why I had felt so different from the other children all those years ago?

At that time, St Vincent School did not have its own swimming pool and we had to walk two or three miles to another school for our swimming lessons. It was a rough path and I found the surface difficult to walk on, often trip-ping and stumbling. Was this because of that poor balance that often goes with Usher syndrome? Sister Fabiola would sometimes ask some of the older pupils to give me a piggy-back rides.

Another incident that came to my mind was having tea at the Jewish Deaf Hostel with a friend when I knocked a large cake flying to the floor as the waitress brought it to our table. I realise now that she was outside my peripheral vision but at the time it was very embarrassing. I also remember Ralph Hahn once waving his hand in front of the bright light of a window to test whether I could see him or not. I could only see the change in the light as he did so. I asked him what he was doing and whether I had a problem with my eyes. He said, 'No.' I asked my father too and he said, 'No.'

Now, with the ophthalmologist's shattering news, I wondered, did they know all along? When I was a teenager, my father had once taken me to a home for deafblind people where he did voluntary work. Why did he do volun-tary work there? He had taken my hand and placed it on the hands of one of the residents and gently shown me how to communicate with him. Why? Were the flashing lights that I saw as I walked home from the cathedral all those years ago connected with my RP? Was that another way that God was already using it to unfold the mystery of my life and direct me along the path to my next journey?

On the way back to South Africa from the USA, I could not make sense of it all. Breaking the news to my cousin Claire, I asked her, 'Why was I born, Claire?' She replied,

'Don't blame your parents, Cyril, and don't give up. I believe you can carry on making your contribution in the world through your blindness.' I have always remembered her words.

However, I feared that my work might be badly threatened. I knew that I must give up my car at once and I was distraught that I might not be able to continue my mission in the more isolated rural regions, and into Zimbabwe, Mozambique, Swaziland and Lesotho.

However, like Claire's, Father Dowling's faith in me did not waver for one moment. He refused to label my disability as a problem. He provided me with a car and a driver. He was always on hand to interpret for me during chapter or community meetings and he made sure I never felt left out of community life. He showed me that human limitations, however serious, do not stand in the way of God's love for His people. This gave me the encouragement I needed to carry on.

Larry Kaufmann was also a source of great support in the years that followed. Little did I know when I had met him for the first time all those years before how that young theology student, who had opened the door of the Redemptorist monastery in Pretoria, would become a lifelong friend to me. Larry became fluent in sign language and often acted as my interpreter as our paths crossed in Cape Town, in the USA and elsewhere in the world. Wherever I travelled in my work, he would make the effort to visit me. From the start of our friendship, he seemed to know that my disability should not undermine my capacity for work as a priest. In fact, he considered it a gift of life from God.

I remember one occasion when he was working in the parish in Grassy Park, Cape Town. He invited me to hear confession, but I made my excuses saying, 'No, no. People would never understand me.' It was my attempt to avoid embarrassment. Larry simply and firmly encouraged me to accept his invitation.

Nervously, I waited in the confessional, recalling awkward experiences years before when I was asked to hear confessions in the cathedral.

Just like now, I had protested, but I was told that it is not so important to know what the people are saying as to be generous with forgiving them. So I had hung a notice on my confessional box that read:

Father Cyril Axelrod (Deaf Priest)

The first visitor that day was a middle-aged woman. By the vibration on my Office Book, I sensed that she spoke with an extremely loud voice. I turned to her putting my finger to my lips, 'Sh! Sh! Sh!' She jumped and exclaimed: 'You're *not* deaf!' Embarrassed, I could not think how to explain. Instead, I blessed her in peace.

A few minutes later, another parishioner came to the confessional. I opened the screen but instead of a face to lipread, I looked straight at a man's chest and a tie. He must have been all of seven feet tall, and in order to look up at his lips I had to remove my chair and lower myself to the floor. He was so concerned by the awkwardness of the situation that two weeks later he returned and handed me a small gift-wrapped parcel. Inside was a small red carpet for me to use whenever I had to sit on the confessional floor to lipread.

This time, things were very different and not what I feared at all. The people entering the confessional were very much at ease. Their smiles reassured me and they all spoke slowly and clearly. I was amazed. After an hour, I came out and said to Father Larry, 'How wonderful. Your people make their confessions so well.' He smiled and just went away without saying a word. Later I discovered that he had been standing outside the confessional to explain to people how to speak to me. How thoughtful Larry has always been towards me.

CHAPTER TWENTY-ONE

South East Asia

When I was at school my teacher, Sister Fabiola, a woman of great serenity, introduced me to some basic Chinese history and shared with me her love of Chinese wisdom. This caught my imagination and started what was to become a voyage of discovery. I also met a Chinese man who worked for my father and he showed me Chinese script and introduced me to Chinese food. I was intrigued by the differences between us and thus began my first understanding of the rich diversity and difference among peoples that has grown steadily in me and guided so much of my life.

Later, as a young priest my interest in Chinese culture was re-kindled when I was invited to dine with a group of Chinese people who told me more about their philosophy and customs. I had no idea that one day in the future I would be working in South East Asia and in China. Neither did I know what a warm welcome and acceptance I would find there, and what an enrichment and broadening of my faith there would be from the people I met there and from their teaching.

Before 1985 I had only preached in South Africa, Europe and the USA. Now Kevin Dowling (then the South African Vice-Provincial Superior) encouraged me to plan a short preaching mission somewhere new. For a year I had been corresponding with Redemptorist students in Singapore, who, in 1980, had set up the Amalgamation of the Deaf Ministry there, in the Novena Church. So when Kevin Dowling suggested a preaching mission I chose Singapore.

During my three months there, I stayed at the Redemptorist Community House, a vast mansion that once belonged to a Malaysian sheikh. It stood on a hill above one of the busiest streets in the city. Next to it was the Novena Church, architecturally a mix of Malaysian and British colonial styles. Every Saturday over 60,000 people attended the hourly novena services there and for deaf people there was a special Mass said outside in the garden under a large canopy that was surrounded by beautiful tropical plants.

My stay in Singapore gave me many new and rich experiences. During the nineteenth century the British colony had attracted migrants from China and India, and consequently was home to a vibrant mix of cultures and peoples. The Chinese way of life and culture continued to inspire me.

I was also introduced, for the first time, to Zen by an Australian Redemptorist, Brother Cassimir, who had been taught by a Benedictine monk in India.

A deeply spiritual man, Brother Cassimir invited me to his home for eight days to pray under his spiritual guidance. The weather was very hot and humid as I travelled by bus away from the busy city centre, through roads lined with small Chinese-owned shops, and on into the leafy residential areas. Brother Cassimir's house was Malaysian with strong Chinese influence. It was set amidst huge green tropical plants and inside it there was a small chapel that was like nothing I had ever seen before. Inside the chapel itself was a pond with a few goldfish or koi, a small fountain and water plants. A little wooden bridge spanned the pond, symbolising the link between earth and heaven and reminding us that we, as people, are the link between earth and God. There were no chairs, just cushions to sit on, and no windows. The only light came from the big spotlight over the fishpond.

Brother Cassimir invited me to sit on the floor like a Buddhist monk. Dressed in a loose cotton shirt and trousers like a Malay, he sat on a large cushion as the teacher of Zen and I sat at his feet like a student. On the floor he lit a small oil lamp and placed incense on charcoal in a small bowl. He bowed to me slowly and spoke for about twenty minutes about the method of Zen prayer. It was a very simple form of contemplation. Then he left me alone in the chapel. I sat motionless on the cushion facing the lamp for forty minutes, gazing at the bright flame and its soft glow. The rhythm of my breathing slowly relaxed my whole body into tranquillity. In stark contrast to the monastic life where monks chant their prayers, there was just a silence, a stillness and a feeling of God's presence within me. For eight days I prayed like this. The power of meditation and this simple form of spirituality showed me a new way to experience God's omnipotent presence within all of us, in the seat of our own consciousness. My life of prayer was forever broadened.

While I was in Singapore, I got to know deaf people both inside and outside the Church. They made me feel at home and gave me many happy memories. I remember one deaf man who had no education whatsoever and could not even communicate in gestures. He was the uncle of one of the volunteers, and although he had attended the church for over fifty years, he had never been allowed to receive Holy Communion because of his lack of religious education. His family felt helpless and I resolved to find a way somehow to enable him to receive God's love through the Holy Communion.

I decided to give him a short two-week Catechism using simple gesture and visual aids. I cut out pictures from magazines of flowers and forests and food and water to show him God's creations. I showed him pictures of things and people he loved to show him God's love for him. It was such a beautiful experience for me, the Sunday before I left Singapore, to bring him to receive Holy Communion for the first time on his sixty-fourth birthday, while his family looked on, filled with emotion. He was illiterate but now was taking part in the service and understanding it. To me it was a real breakthrough that there were other ways for deaf people to get life experience and understanding outside formal education.

I also began to realise that in Singapore at the time there was a rift in the deaf community between the Catholic deaf and a group of 'born again' Christians. The vice-president of the Deaf Association was very concerned and approached me to ask whether I could help bring the two groups together. A week before I left Singapore he invited me to come to a joint meeting of the two groups to encourage them to have a sense of belonging to one deaf family, regardless of their creeds. Remarkably, they responded positively, and felt liberated by the idea of this religious freedom within a stronger deaf community.

A week later, in a touching gesture, they flocked to the airport together to bid me farewell. I owed them all an immense debt, for in their gentle acceptance I had found inspiration. My determination to work with deaf people in South East Asia or in China was cemented.

Such was the bond that I had made with deaf people in Singapore that ten years later, when I returned there to celebrate the silver jubilee of my priesthood with the same Redemptorist community and the same deaf friends, deaf people greeted me at the airport with a placard saying 'Welcome Father Cyril'. A huge deaf congregation packed into the chapel, sitting together on the carpeted floor. The deaf choir signed the hymns and the Lord's Prayer, the silent Mass was conducted entirely in Singapore Sign Language and the deaf community had organised an informal reception for me on the monastery patio after the service. It was a clear, hot day and the sun shone down on those I had come to love so much.

When I returned to South Africa in 1985 after my first mission to Singapore I already knew for sure that I wanted to work in South East Asia. I was most disappointed when the Vice-Provincial Superior advised me that it was too early for me to make such a decision. He wanted me to take time for patient reflection and discernment. First he sent me to work with a group of hearing theology students living on a farm near Durban and then later to take care of two elderly Redemptorist priests in the last days of their lives in The Monastery in Cape Town. These were bleak years for me and at times I felt as if God had deserted me. I was unclear what He wanted of me but I resigned myself to His will.

During these years I had recurring dreams that God was calling me to Chinese deaf people despite my deteriorating vision and despite my ties with the South African deaf community.

Around Easter in 1988, Father Dowling, who had by now been transferred to work in Rome, accompanied the Father General from Rome, Father Juan Lasso de la Vega, on an official visit to South Africa. The Father General spoke at a meeting about the need for new Redemptorist missions to be set up to serve the poor and abandoned in other parts of the world. I sat through the meeting with a heavy heart but at lunch the Father General approached me and, with one of my confrères interpreting for him, he said, 'I have heard of your wonderful work in Singapore. Are you interested in a mission to China?' My mind went blank. For several years I had thought of nothing else but now all I could think of was my deteriorating eyesight and the deaf people I would be leaving behind in South Africa.

But Father Dowling and the deaf community knew that it was God's call for me to go, and gave me their full support. The Father General said that my failing eyesight was not my problem. It was God's problem. So began my next journey - my journey to the East.

I started with a two-weeks ministry in Singapore. Then on 4 September 1988 I headed for Hong Kong, where for the first year I was to be based with the American Maryknoll missionary order, an arrangement that had been set up for me by Father Larry Kaufmann. They had agreed that I should be affiliated to them while I explored the region to find the most suitable place for my mission. I arrived to a warm welcome from the Maryknoll priests Fathers Eugene Thalman, Juan Zuniga and Charlie Dittmeier, and also from the teachers and deaf children from the Canossian School for the Deaf, a large elementary school. The children had been told that a deaf priest from the 'Black continent' would be arriving and were shocked when they saw I had a white skin. So they called me the 'White Devil'.

Over the next few weeks Father Michael McKieran helped me to get acclimatised. He was seventy years old and had spent a number of years in China before the Communists came to power in 1950 and deported him. He shared with me his knowledge of Chinese culture and philosophy, of Chinese 'wit and wisdom'. He introduced me to his old Chinese friend, a religious teacher of faith who later 'christened' me in Chinese 'Father Chan Man On', which means 'peace for people'. I felt most honoured to receive this most elegant of names, and in the end I was known throughout the region as Chan Man On by both the hearing and the deaf people.

Father Charlie also introduced me to a language school so that I could study Cantonese, but I was turned away because of my deafness. Instead, the Principal of the Canossian School for the Deaf arranged for me to have private tuition every week to support the study that I did on my own in my room. I was taught in a very methodical way. My jaw used to ache from practising the different tones of Cantonese. My head became dizzy from memorising the 314 radical roots of Chinese characters. My hand became stiff from writing one character over and over again until the page was full. I felt like an eleventh-century monk writing scripture in his cell for hours each day. However, my teacher encouraged me by saying 'Patience in making strokes step by step makes a person a good Chinese!'

During my year there Father Charlie Dittmeier and I travelled out of Hong Kong to Taiwan, the Philippines, and Macau – searching for somewhere to base our work. In each place the social and political environments were different and so were the needs of the deaf people that we met. Singapore had always been my first choice, but I knew that God had different plans for me. At first it looked as if Hong Kong would become the place of my mission. The deaf people there were very anxious to have me. Then I went for a week's retreat in Macau, and that changed the direction of my life.

CHAPTER TWENTY-TWO

Macau

I arrived alone at the busy port of Macau, which is situated on a peninsula at the estuary of the Pearl River.

Day and night, ferry boats and jetfoils come and go there every fifteen minutes, making the hundred-kilometre crossing from Hong Kong. I was immediately struck by the amazing blend of Portuguese and Chinese culture and architecture. I learned that the Macau around the ferry port is a modern mecca for visitors, especially those coming for its gambling casinos, horse and dog races and nightlife. Sometimes called the 'Monte Carlo of the East', six million Hong Kong residents and foreign tourists flock to the city each year.

Then I ventured into the city and further afield to the islands. Everywhere there is Portuguese influence and history. Beautiful colonial buildings line many streets. Portuguese churches date back to the sixteenth century and house medieval paintings. With a population of over 450,000, Macau is even more densely populated than Hong Kong. Indeed it has more people per square mile that any other place in the world. Its streets are thronged with people, cars, motorcycles and rickshaws. This would become a challenge for me with my failing eyesight.

The mix of races and cultures intrigued me while the mix of Western and Oriental taste in architecture, food and religion were unlike anything I had known. Although often called 'the Catholic City' because of the Portuguese influence, Catholics are very much a minority and throughout the year festivals and processions of many different religions take place in the streets. Since the sixteenth century Macau had been a Portuguese colony and would remain so until 1999 when it was to be handed back to the People's Republic of China.

Next I crossed the bridge to Coloane, one of Macau's two main islands, where nineteenth-century fishermen's houses look out over the South China Sea and across to the mountains of China. Chinese junks and Portuguese fishing boats share the same waters and along the shore fishermen's nets were laid out for mending and cleaning and fish were hung up to dry in the sun. I had seen nothing like it before. I stayed on the island for two weeks in the Canossian Convent to reflect a while on what God wanted of me.

Macau, unlike Hong Kong, had no specialist services for deaf people. There was only an integrated service for disabled people that was not meeting the needs of *deaf* people. Gradually the answer became clear and I knew that here in Macau, amidst the many cultures, races, religions and languages, God wanted me to set up my mission for deaf people.

And so, on 1 October 1989, Bishop Domingo Lam, the first Chinese bishop of Macau, accepted my services to the deaf people of his diocese and a formal announcement was made in the Government Gazette. I moved from the Convent into a room in Father Mario's rectory, still on the island and with views out to sea, and each day I would travel by bus across the long bridge to the mainland.

I started my work in the centre for disabled people, under an American nun, Sister Arlene. There, blind people, physically and mentally disabled people and deaf people were integrated together. It was a year during which I had to make many adaptations. I had to start getting accustomed to the Chinese culture and to get to know the deaf people in the centre who were making clothes and craftwork for sale. As I began to learn Chinese Sign Language deaf people started to confide in me and tell how they felt they were regarded as uneducated citizens, hardly better than beggars, and how they dreamed of having a centre of their own. I also met parents of deaf children and I soon began to understand that disabled children in China were considered 'bad luck', and an embarrassment to their families. The parents would often keep them indoors, hidden away from society, sometimes not telling the authorities of their existence. I realised there was a great deal of work to be done.

My first project was to develop a hearing and speech clinic in a small room at the centre. Sister Arlene gave her blessing but I had to find the finance to support the teachers, buy equipment and set up a training programme for parents to learn to communicate with their deaf children. My main aim was to help parents see their deaf children as bringers of hope, not bad luck. Unfortunately, when Sister Arlene was recalled to America we ran into difficulties. The Government considered our unit outside the remit of the centre because it was regarded as educational rather than as a Social Service and I was asked to leave.

Although this was an enormous blow, God stood by me. I had been almost on the point of giving up when a deaf man saved me. Ao Chi San came to me and signed a 'thumbs down' followed by a 'thumbs up' and then wrote in Chinese an old proverb: 'Never say that you will fail and you will succeed.' With this he restored my sagging spirits and gave me fresh courage.

I was offered a temporary room in central Macau by Caritas, one of the largest Catholic organisations in the world, specialising in development, relief and social service. It was a time of great struggle because the room was too small for the dozen or so deaf and hearing-impaired children that now attended the Speech and Language Centre. We had only two teachers, very basic furniture and teaching resources, and no modern equipment.

In 1991 Caritas offered me a second room in their building to establish a second centre, the Social Services Centre for the Deaf. Both rooms were so cramped that it was difficult for us to develop the work of either service fully. Nevertheless, the teachers' confidence grew steadily and the only speech therapist in Macau, Maria Albino, who was

Macanese (Macau-born), was a great support to me. A final year social work student, Judy Leong Hok Un, also visited me regularly and finally came to join our team. She knew little about deafness at first but rolled up her sleeves and got stuck in at once. I taught the welfare workers sign language and deaf awareness and then we were able to offer some basic literacy and numeracy skills to deaf adults.

Then a remarkable deaf woman joined us. She would prove to be a most supportive colleague, an inspiring teacher to me of Chinese wisdom and ultimately an important leader. Alice Lao Iok Ieng gave up a higher wage in a textile factory to come and work with us. She had grown up in Guangzhou in China, and received a good education until the Cultural Revolution interrupted it. Confined to her home between 1965 and 1975 and hungry for knowledge, she educated herself with Chinese classics, Shakespeare and Aristotle. Having followed the teachings of Mao, she was committed to the vision of community work. With this determination and background, she became a wonderful role model to other deaf people. She worked tirelessly with them encouraging them to work together and to help each other. She always responded eagerly to my encouragement to broaden her own horizons and those of other deaf people.

There were many ups and downs, particularly because we had so little space. My vision was also slowly failing and sometimes I felt like a ship sailing on rough seas. But God's guidance was miraculous. Bishop Lam remained steadfast in his belief and faith in me. The Father General of the Redemptorist order who had sent me there in the first place

173

came to visit. He was convinced that it was God's plan for me to be there and this gave me great strength. When Father Michael Fish, the newly elected Provincial Superior from South Africa, came to see my work he promised the deaf people of Macau that he would not take me away from them. Cheers of excitement followed and this reaffirmed my feeling that Macau was indeed the place that had been chosen for me.

At the end of 1991 my godfather and friend, Robert Simmons, came from South Africa to see me for Christmas. We spent a week together in Hong Kong visiting the Canossian School for the Deaf and the Association of the Deaf. We had discussions with them there about meeting the needs of deafblind people and this was later to become the start of a new project for me. Robert was amazed by how well I had mastered written and some spoken Mandarin, Cantonese and Portuguese, and also that I had acquired a smattering of other Chinese languages.

Back in Macau on Christmas Eve, I celebrated Mass in Chinese Sign Language with Robert in attendance.

He was enormously encouraging about our work there and suggested that it needed recognising and endorsing by the Government now, so that we could really move forward and expand the service. This was to lead to the beginning of my dialogue with the Social Welfare Department. Two years later they began to share my goals of establishing a centre for the deaf people of Macau. After lengthy and gentle negotiations I was given rooms in northern Macau and a Portuguese lawyer helped me draw up a constitution for the Macau Deaf Association. An inaugural announcement was made on 4

August 1994 and at last the dream of the deaf community of Macau had become a reality. The Kai Chung Centre was established.

My aim had always been for the Macau Deaf Association to become a strong, self-governing, non-profit-making, non-denominational organisation run by deaf people, which could administer the Speech and Language Skills Centre for Hearing-Impaired Children and the Social Services Centre for the Deaf. It was essential to me that the Association be independent from both the Church and the Portuguese government because I was determined that the services should survive after the eventual handover of Macau back to the People's Republic of China in 1999. That, together with raising public awareness of our work, tackling the stigma that was still attached to deafness and developing services for deafblind people, was my next challenge.

From time to time I travelled away from Macau for short periods. In 1994 I visited the Philippines and found the deaf community there was run by one man and had very few facilities. A year later while I was in Vienna in Austria for the World Federation of the Deaf Congress, the director of the Secretariat for the Asia-Pacific region told me of his concerns about the Philippines. I volunteered to go back to there to encourage the deaf community to develop itself with a formal structure and a coordinated national organisation that would be in line with the World Federation. When I had finished, I went back to Macau leaving their newly elected committee to work out their constitution and to get local groups and clubs to affiliate.

A few years later the first Assembly of the Christian

Philippine Federation of the Deaf took place and I was named as one of their founders. To me, it was a wonderful moment. It was like giving birth and watching my child grow.

I also visited mainland China and learned of deaf people's experiences there, and a Chinese delegation came to see our work in Macau. I worked closely, as a volunteer, with the Hong Kong Society for the Blind and, together with two of the staff at the Society, I went to the USA for a six-week leadership programme on deafblindness at the Perkins School for the Blind in Boston and in the Helen Keller International Center in New York. This was my first introduction to tactile sign language for the deafblind.

We were able to bring back what we had learned to Hong Kong where we developed a training programme of our own for deafblind adults and children. The programme had to be sensitive to the cultural needs of the Chinese, who preferred to be visited discreetly in their homes rather than be trained in centres, and we also needed to adapt the tactile sign language to accommodate the Chinese written characters and the Chinese custom that dictates that it is not respectful to touch each other. Eventually we were able to produce a video of over 1,000 characters that showed how to use the deafblind person's hands when signing. We hoped this could be used not only in Hong Kong and Macau but also in China and elsewhere in South East Asia.

Back at the Macau Deaf Association I had another project in hand. I was the Executive Director but my aim was to have other deaf people ready to take roles of responsibility before my sight failed completely and before the handover of Macau back to China. With this in mind, in 1994, two professors came from Gallaudet University USA to provide some leadership training for deaf people. Two years later I took eight of the deaf committee members and staff, including Alice, over to Gallaudet for the second part of the training programme.

It was while we were there that I was rushed to hospital with a thrombosis in my leg and was advised to remain in Washington for the next three months. My deaf colleagues were dismayed that they would have to return to Macau without me as their mentor. I too had misgivings about relinquishing my responsibilities. For three months I could only direct them by letter but I knew that in my absence the time was right for them to develop independence and confidence and begin running the Association.

Two years after I returned to Macau some of the long, hard struggles seemed to be coming to an end, for we were able to move to larger premises. Ten rooms had become available above an indoor fruit, vegetable and fish market, and with the support of the government we were able to relocate there. At last our patience had been rewarded. We had gained recognition and could go forward with our service. We improved our facilities, created a library, and with the generous donation of computers, printers and scanners from the Lions' Club, we were able to press ahead with vocational training for young deaf adults, a new adult literacy training programme, social and occupational activities and a sign language interpreter service. Watched by the entire deaf community and various dignitaries, the Governor of Macau unveiled the plaque to mark the official opening of the new

177

Social Services Centre for Deaf People in August 1999. It was a momentous occasion.

My eyesight finally forced me to resign my position as Executive Director of the Macau Deaf Association, but what joy it was to me to have witnessed the profound changes for deaf people in Macau during my twelve-year mission there. It was the right time to resign as it was time to hand over the reins to the deaf people there.

Some months before, I had received the biggest honour of all from the deaf world in recognition of my work. I had taken a group of deaf people from Macau to the World Federation of the Deaf Congress in Brisbane, Australia, in order that they should meet officers from deaf associations around the world. I had no idea that my name had been put forward, and I had already been selected, for the prestigious award of a First Class International Social Medal for distinguished work for the international promotion of the human rights of deaf people.

I was overcome with emotion as I was led on to the stage and the president paid tribute to my work among deaf people, not only in Macau but also in the Philippines, Singapore, and Hong Kong and in South Africa, as well as to my missions in the USA, England and Europe. I still had enough sight at that time to see the applause as the audience of three thousand deaf people raised their hands in the air to wave their appreciation and congratulation, as is the deaf custom.

34. Singapore. An evening celebration, 1985.

35. A farewell from the Singapore deaf people at the airport, 1985.

36. With deaf children at the Speech and Language Centre, Macau, 1991.

37. Tea Ceremony at a wedding in Hong Kong, 1992.

181

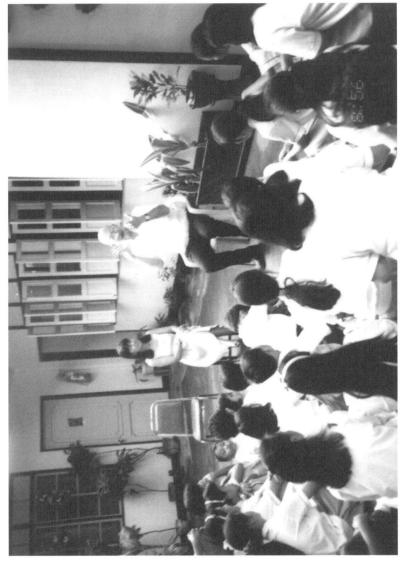

38. Talking to a group of deaf pupils at St Augustine School for the Deaf, near Manila, Philippines, 1995.

39. In the People's Republic of China, at The Great Wall,
with Simon Chan Wai Hung, Alice Lao Iok Ieng and
Noven Li Yuk Lin. 1999.

40. At work with the Board of the Macau Deaf Association.

41. Demonstrating to the Governor of Macau the computers
donated by the Lions' Club. 1999.

42. With the Governor of Macau for the unveiling of the plaque to mark the official opening of the new Social Services Centre for Deaf People in Macau, August 1999.

185

43. Farewell from the deaf people of Macau and Hong Kong. Hong Kong, 1999.

CHAPTER TWENTY-THREE

England

By the time Portugal handed Macau back to the People's Republic of China in 1999, it had been nearly nineteen years since the diagnosis of my Usher syndrome. My eyesight had steadily deteriorated and by then my visual acuity was very poor. My field of vision had decreased to about 3 per cent of normal and I could not see in the dark at all.

It was while I was still in South Africa that my lateral peripheral vision had started to close in and a few years later I noticed the upper and lower vision was receding. When people signed to me I found that their hands seemed to disappear outside my field of vision and I had to move my head up and down and sideways to keep their signing in my visual frame and to be able to see obstacles in my path. I had already started to use a red and white cane.

Shortly after arriving in Macau, I noticed white spots, or floaters, in front of my eyes. A year later blank areas appeared like tiny explosions around the edges of my vision, which were caused by the retinal cells dying off. The peripheral vision continued to close in and I started bumping into, and tripping over, things more often. My three-dimensional vision became somewhat distorted and my sense of distance altered, making it difficult for me to locate things. My right eye deteriorated faster than my left, which caused further distortion. Gradually, the floaters became larger and moon-shaped, and my central vision changed as a whitish fog seemed to form over both my eyes like veils that became thicker and greyer as time went by.

One very special man had seen how my sight was changing and became an important source of support to me. I first met Simon Chan Wai Hung in Hong Kong where he acted as a voluntary sign language interpreter for me. On many occasions he then came to Macau to help me with Mass. We became firm friends. I was able to confide in him and he was a most sensitive listener. Although he did not know anything about deafblindness he was not afraid of it. He took up the challenge to learn and even went on a two-week course in Seattle, USA. He always made the time to guide me when I went to unknown places and was with me as an interpreter when Alice and I went to Beijing. He has since become a trusted guide on some of my European and American travels.

My time in Macau was coming to a close. It was time for the independent Deaf Association to be self-governing, and for the deaf people to take over and move things forward under the new Chinese government. My eyesight also meant that my role was over and my mission in China was at an end. God had other plans for me, but as I felt the darkness enveloping me, I had no idea what they were.

I arrived in the United Kingdom in 2000. I could still read with the use of a magnifier but, before long, I could only see the shape of people. Their faces lacked definition - no eyes, nose, mouth any longer, only the shape of the head like a photo negative. Soon I could only distinguish between light and dark.

I became depressed, angry and filled with disbelief. It was a time of great loss and I seemed to feel it throughout my whole body. I became restless, weary and uncoordinated. My vision, my physical mobility, my ability to read, my ability to communicate with others and above all, my independence, had all changed. The roots of my love were with the Chinese people, their way of life, their culture and their deaf community, and yet I had left my job and my friends. God had brought me instead to an unfamiliar country where everything was completely new to me.

Only a few people knew my background or knew of my life's service. Suddenly I was seen only as a deafblind man. People did not approach me as they once had. I had learned to receive sign language by feeling rather than watching the signer's hands (hands-on), but I noticed that some deaf people in England seemed to withdraw from me, not feeling confident about communicating with me this way; or maybe because they did not know me before I was blind.

My work with deaf people in so many countries that had so fulfilled me seemed taken away from me. I felt quite lost.

Most of all, I felt I was leaving my community, the deaf community, as I became not deaf but deafblind. It all seemed too much for me to bear. How could I possibly continue with my priesthood?

In fact, it was the beginning of a new journey. It was a journey that I knew I must walk by faith alone. I had no idea what God could possibly have in mind for me, but I knew I had to go on.

* * *

My first destination was Rainbow Court, a training centre run by Deafblind UK in Peterborough, an hour and a half north of London. Filled with trepidation, I was reminded of how I had felt when I first went to China when everything was so new to me. Now I had the darkness as well as the silence to endure and the challenges I faced were completely unknown.

I knew I must find the hope and courage to go through this most important next step, somehow. I knew I must learn new skills for my mobility and for my communication. I knew I must trust in God to show me the way to a new kind of fulfilment and a new way of using my deafblindness in the service of others.

For three months I stayed at St Peter and All Souls presbytery in Peterborough and went every day for intensive rehabilitation training at Deafblind UK. I learned to receive communication through the deafblind manual alphabet where a sighted person writes or spells on to the hands of a deafblind person. This has since proved useful to me in my communication with my guides when out shopping, at conferences and at religious meetings. I learned to be guided and also how to use my red and white cane to the full, moving it from side to side across my path to 'scan' for obstacles. I was taught how to manoeuvre round corners with my cane and to walk between two parallel white lines. I learned to identify slopes and to recognise different surfaces - smooth, rough, bumpy, grass, and sand - and to assess the width of the pavement by feeling the wall and then the kerb with my cane. I learned to distinguish with my cane between telegraph poles, lampposts and road signs by their circumferences.

I also received training in independent living skills in a specially designed training room. I was shown how to move around the room and use the raised Braille dots on the cooker, microwave, washing machine and dishwasher. I learned to identify the different shapes and sizes of crockery, kitchen utensils and cutlery, as well as to put them in places where they could be easily found again. I learned how to time the cooking of foods and how to move the food to the centre of my plate so that I could scoop it on to the fork or spoon and into my mouth. I acquired a neat device that could be placed on the rim of a cup, with a pad that vibrated against my finger when I had poured in enough liquid.

I was shown how to organise clothes in a wardrobe by the feel of the fabric and the type of the garment. A large piece of stiff paper on a hanger could separate clothes of different colours and different shaped buttons could be sewn on the bottom of shirts to show how formal or casual a garment was. I learned that in the bathroom I had to sit rather than stand at the toilet. Furniture had always to be kept in the same position so I knew where it was and could use it to orientate myself as I moved about. I learned how to use a pager that had different vibrations to indicate the doorbell, the fire alarm, or the text telephone, which I could use through a Braille reader. When I later got a flat of my own I still sometimes made mistakes. Once, two firemen turned up at my door. I was blissfully unaware that my cooking had set the smoke alarm off.

I also learned how to book the disabled service for rail travellers, so rail staff could assist me at the station and guide me to my seat on the train, or from my train seat to my next connection. In time, I would become a frequent deafblind traveller and that would lead to some unexpected adventures. Once, I found myself in Wolverhampton rather than Birmingham, and another time I was mistakenly bundled into a taxi instead of my waiting train. I did not know where I was, but I soon found out by asking the station staff to spell block capitals on the palm of my hand. Sometimes it was almost too much for strangers to comprehend that I could be travelling alone. I could almost sense their astonishment when they found out that I was a priest and that I had worked all over the world. People could see my disability but they could not always see the man inside. They could see my deafblindness but not my capabilities.

I learned how to use a Braille watch to tell the time. That too has led to some amusing incidents like the occasion when I was staying with friends at a cottage. I misread my Braille watch and went downstairs to breakfast far too early and almost went flying over one of my friends who was asleep on a camp bed in the living room.

These were all part of the huge adaptation I had to make as I became a fully deafblind person. The hardest thing of all was learning Braille. I had to find a new sensitivity in my fingertips. In the early weeks it felt an uphill struggle as my fingers tried to make sense of the tiny raised dots. They seemed as alien as the Chinese characters did when I first so painstakingly learned them in Macau. At times, I felt I would burst with the frustration of it, but I counselled myself with patience and perseverance, remembering the old Chinese proverb that the deaf man had given me in Macau: 'Never say that you will fail and you will succeed.'

The experience also reminded me of when I had spent ten days on a Buddhist retreat at a farm south of Durban after I had come back from Singapore. Each day I had to weed a bed in the gardens by hand. I had to sit on the ground for one hour pulling each small weed out, one by one by one, for this was an exercise to develop patience. How I valued that now. I had already mastered eight different sign languages and the basics of seven spoken languages, plus some Yiddish, in order to communicate with others. It was Braille though, that was to become my lifeline, the most important communication tool of all. For without it, how would I have access to the written word again and how would I communicate with those who cannot sign or use the deafblind manual alphabet?

Slowly, slowly, I began to acquire the basics of the new skills that I needed, and in time I was able to read my first Braille book. I was also able to access files, emails and world news on my computer, through a Braille reading device

193

attached to it, even if it did take more than twice as long as reading the printed word. I never dreamt I would later while away evenings rediscovering my Hebrew through Braille. Who knows, maybe it will be Cantonese next, although for a deaf man that could be a struggle, because the dots in Chinese Braille represent the sounds of the language and not the characters.

I also began to feel comfortable using communicator/guides who could lead me where I wanted to go and assist me in communication., but, I failed to see how I could continue my life of service. After my three months' training I still felt that I stood before a locked door without a key.

I went to stay in a Redemptorist community house in Clapham, London, for five months, hoping that the future would become clear to me. It was a devastating time. No one there could communicate with me, or knew what going blind meant to me. I felt quite alone and often stayed in my room with only my laptop computer and my Braille-reader as a means of communication with my friends around the world and with my dear cousin, Dawn, in South Africa.

One day, a priest friend from the house decided to go out for a long walk. I asked if I could go with him but he seemed frightened by the idea of taking me, a deafblind man, with him into the busy streets of London. Suddenly the anger, frustration and anxiety that had been building up in my 'solitary confinement' welled up and spilled out as tears of sorrow. Shocked by this, my friend suddenly realised how I must feel and his attitude towards me changed. Without discussion or question, he seemed to see deafblindness in a new light and after that he would often accompany me on

194

walks or visits to places of interest. That companionship meant a lot to me.

However, I was still not getting the full support I needed in the community house and I would pour out my feelings to Deafblind UK by email. Eventually, they wrote to me and offered me a one-bedroom flat in Rainbow Court, which was their sheltered accommodation for deafblind people.

This move back to Peterborough in November 2000 did not seem like a complete solution to me. I resented the idea of dependency and at first I felt that people might not always be able to see what I was capable of. Nevertheless, the move did give me some support and time to reflect on how I could find a way to fulfil my life again. I was journeying into the world of deafblindness and I needed to explore the dark empty space in my heart and touch the unknown, from where I felt sure somewhere God was calling me. It continued to be a time of suffering for me, of darkness, silence and isolation. Frustration and despair weighed upon my shoulders. Yet there were times when I was able to reflect on sad and happy moments in my life and these memories were a great consolation to me, and a source of inner healing. It was also a time of mystery and discovery as I learned to understand the true meaning of blindness. I began to 'feel' blindness in a new way as the true touch of God upon my soul. I began to make blindness my friend. I could see that I was beginning to gain a new kind of knowledge and understanding and wisdom that I could, in turn, give to the world. But I could not quite see how!

Then, just when I was at my lowest, my life's journey started to take on a new direction. Completely out of the blue came news of my honorary doctorate from Gallaudet University. This recognition could not have come at a better time. It was indeed such an honour to me and, what is more, it restored my belief that nothing could take my life's work away from me. The moment I realised that the audience at the Gallaudet University ceremony had erupted into a standing ovation for my work, which I felt through my whole body, I knew that I still had many things to do. This was not the end but a new beginning. That was why I had gone to England - to serve deafblind people. On my journey home I felt uplifted. I knew that my blindness was no longer going to be a barrier to me, either in my work or in my worldwide travels.

Shortly after my return from the USA I was delighted when Deafblind UK offered me a voluntary post as their 'Pastoral Support Development Coordinator'. It was an excellent opportunity for me. The aim of the job was to promote awareness of the needs of deafblind people in churches and places of worship around the United Kingdom, regardless of denomination. This work led me to meet with the Archbishop of Canterbury, Catholic bishops, other religious leaders as well as members of the Jewish Deaf Association. My role was to encourage the development of pastoral care for deafblind people within those churches and places of worship and to encourage full access to public worship with full participation for deafblind people. Part of the job was also to facilitate training programmes for ministers and religious leaders and workshops for pastoral care, and to encourage the transcription of printed news, sermons and reading material into Braille or large print.

Also in 2002 I was elected to the Board of Directors at Deafblind UK. This was another great honour. As the only deafblind person on the board who used sign language, I hoped that I might raise the profile of 'hands-on' tactile sign language, which is preferred by many people who have Usher syndrome. How fortunate that I had learned sign language. It is readily adaptable to a tactile form. How different my adjustment would have been if I had not, or if I had been born blind and then lost my hearing. I also saw being on the Board as an opportunity to encourage leadership and independence in deafblind people, especially those who are born deaf and then acquire blindness.

At the same time, I also decided to embark on a completely new challenge. I decided to study aromatherapy massage. This seemed to me one way that I could offer a service to deafblind people. I felt I could use the tactile approach of massage to give comfort to those who might often be very isolated, lonely and anxious, and I knew that the oils could improve health and well-being. I have learned through experience how important touch is for deafblind people, not only as a means of guiding and communicating, but also as means of support and human contact. Massage was not entirely new to me. In China, I had been interested in Chinese medicine and therapies. I had already studied and practised Chinese massage and learned something of t'ai chi as well.

So I approached Peterborough Regional College. An interview with a tutor was arranged and I went along on the day with a communicator/guide to assist me. At first the tutor tried to discourage me. She saw my disability and she thought the course would be too difficult for me. It was then that Deafblind UK came to the rescue pointing out to them what assistance I could have. Very soon I was enrolled on a part-time course with two support workers, one to take notes and one to interpret to me during lectures using the deaf-blind manual alphabet on my hands. The service they and the college's Sensory Support Team gave me was superb. They converted teaching notes into Braille and assisted me with reviewing my assignments.

To make it easier I decided to take the course over two years and to study the massage in the first year and aromatherapy in the second. During the lectures I would try to memorise what was spelled on to my hands and then later I would go through the notes in my own time. When the tutor needed to demonstrate a massage technique to the students she would often choose me as the guinea pig so that I could learn not by seeing her do it but by feeling it on my own body. When it was my turn to give a treatment she would place her hands on mine, directing me how to make the correct movements. While the other students sat tests or examinations in an hour or two, I was allowed to sit in another room and was given three hours to do it, to allow my interpreter, Janette Olive, to fingerspell the questions and write down my answers as I voiced them to her. Back in my flat, I would spend hours studying or writing an assignment on my computer, which would then be emailed to Janette for proofreading before it was handed in. I even had to do an oral examination with an interpreter fingerspelling every word. I found it extremely challenging but at the same time very rewarding. The support I received from other students, from tutors and from the clients was amazing. Once they knew how determined I was they all believed I would succeed, and that gave me the confidence I needed.

At the end of the two years I received the nationally recognised qualification that has since enabled me to practise in a specially established massage room at Deafblind UK. In recognition of my achievement and the challenges to studying that I had undergone, I also received the Adult Learner's Award. My positive experience has meant that Peterborough Regional College now feels confident about enrolling other deafblind people on courses.

I feel that in some small way my achievements at college may have helped others see that, with the right assistance, deafblind people can take control of their own lives, their own decisions and their own roles. Most people's view of deafblindness is that it is unspeakable, unthinkable, unimaginable. For me it has become a new way of life and one that has offered a new direction. There are frustrations to overcome but many new joys to experience and many new challenges. In some ways, my deafblindness has become the best teacher in my life.

There are challenges too for hearing sighted people who meet or work with deafblind people. To fear deafblindness gets in the way of seeing the opportunities, seeing the rewards, seeing beyond the disability to the person. To support a deafblind person sympathetically and to guide them or communicate for them is an enormous help towards their independence. However, the really rewarding challenge is to see how a deafblind person can, with that assistance, fulfil their own hopes and aspirations, and make their own decisions, at a deeper level of independence.

And so it is that my work here in England as a fully deaf-blind man is only just beginning. After a long period of patient waiting, my path has become clear. With my new qualifications and with the recent launch at London's Westminster Cathedral of my new ministry to deafblind people, God has given me the direction I needed and the chance to continue my life's work. At the same time, He has blessed me with the support services and with the spiritual guidance that I need as a deafblind person and as a priest. I have hopes for a new understanding of deafblindness and of deafblind people and the contribution they can make to the world, and now I can work towards these hopes through the new roles that I have been given. A new journey is beginning.

44. Two deaf delegates, Lindsay Sunne from South Africa and John Chan representing China, place the doctoral hood over my shoulders. Gallaudet University, Washington DC, USA, 2001.

45. Receiving my Honorary Doctorate from I. King Jordan, President of the University.

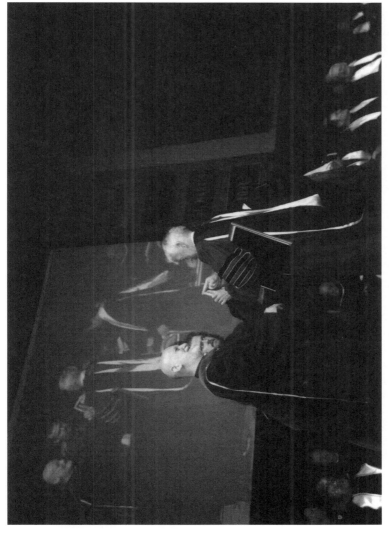

46. President I. King Jordan signs on my hands. Behind us the ceremony is projected onto a large screen so that the deaf audience can see the signing.

203

47. With Steven Walker, staff interpreter for deafblind people, and Dr. Donalda K. Ammons, Professor of Foreign Languages at Gallaudet University.

48. Blessing the Turf for a new building at Deafblind UK. Peterborough, UK. 2001

MASSAGE – Father Cecil using his talents to help others

Healing hands of deafblind priest

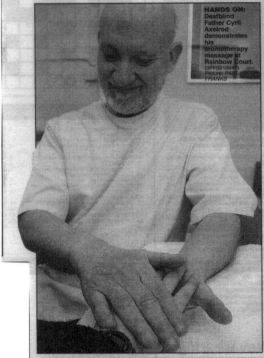

HANDS ON: Deafblind Father Cyril Axelrod demonstrates his aromatherapy massage at Rainbow Court. (3PF0210045) *Picture: PAUL FRANKS*

IRENA BARKER NEWS REPORTER

HE is deaf and blind, but a Catholic priest is using his healing hands to help others.

Talented Father Cyril Axelrod (60) has set up his own professional surgery in the city, to bring the benefits of stimulating aromatherapy massage to people from all walks of life.

Father Cyril qualified as a masseur last year at Peterborough Regional College, and is due to finish a year-long course in aromatherapy this spring.

Father Cyril overcame his own handicaps to learn massage as a way of helping others in the same situation.

He said: "Aromatherapy massage can help relieve the deep pain and frustration of losing your sight, and encourages contact between people – it has an incredible healing power.

"It's important for deaf-blind people to practise it as well. It raises awareness and helps people develop a sense of worth."

Father Cyril first developed his interest in aromatherapy after learning reiki – a type of holistic therapy – when working with deaf people in China.

After coming to the UK two and a half years ago to learn Braille at the city's Deafblind UK training centre, he decided to develop his skills.

Father Cyril said: "It has taken me longer to train than most people, as all the course notes have to be translated into Braille before I can read them.

"But I have an excellent tutor – Jaqueline Miller – who uses her hands to show me the different techniques involved."

In order to give massages, Father Cyril has set up his own massage room at the Deafblind UK National Rehabilitation and Training Centre at Rainbow Court, in Paston Ridings, Peterborough.

He said: "I don't just do massages on deafblind people, I've had a lot of interest from people without disabilities wanting a massage."

Val Stokes, manager of the Deafblind UK training centre, said: "What Cyril is doing is fantastic.

"It sends out a really positive message to people.

"It's an outstanding achievement for him – he's a really incredible man."

irena.barker@peterboroughnow.co.uk

Degrees in philosophy and theology

FATHER Cyril Axelrod is the only deafblind priest in the world.

Originally from South Africa, he has degrees in philosophy and theology from United States universities.

During his career, he has spent time working with deprived children in Soweto, and devoted 12 years of his life to working with young deaf people in Macau.

He only lost his sight completely 15 months ago, but came to Britain to learn Braille after learning about Deafblind UK on the internet.

He now tours the country advising churches on how they can help deafblind people get involved in the church.

49. A newspaper cutting from the Peterborough Evening Telegraph, 2003.

50. A conversation with Sister Chris CFS,
at St John the Evangelist Church, Islington, London, 2004.

207

51. Mass for the Brentwood Deaf Community at St Mary and
St Ethelburga Church, Barking, London, 2004.

52. A conversation with HRH The Princess Royal at the Sense Awards, London. 2004.

53. A return visit to the Deaf Community of Cape Town,
September 2004. Stephen Lombard and I are in front of the plaque
to commemorate the opening in 1994.

54. A Communion service at the Deaf Community of Cape Town
during the same visit. 2004.

55. A Communion service at the Deaf Community of Cape Town
during the same visit. 2004.

56. With Bishop Bernard Longley. Mass at Westminster Cathedral, London, to celebrate the launch of my Ministry to Deafblind People. November 2004.

57. With Bishop Bernard, incensing the altar at the Mass, Westminster Cathedral, London. 27 November 2004.

58. At St John the Evangelist Church, Islington, London,
wearing my Redemptorist habit, black with a white collar. 2004.

CHAPTER TWENTY–FOUR

And the Journey Begins

In February 2002, my cousin Dawn invited me to South Africa to celebrate my sixtieth birthday. With two friends from England to guide me and to provide hands-on interpreting, I flew first to Cape Town for a few days and then on to Johannesburg where Dawn and her husband Steve had arranged a big party in their garden for me.

I was astonished by the changes I was told about. It was quite a different South Africa from the one I had left. Since then, there had been dramatic political changes with the abolition of apartheid and I felt as if I was walking into a new country.

It was such a pleasure for me to revisit the now flourishing Deaf Community of Cape Town with whom I had worked almost twenty years before. When I met my old friend, Wilma Newhoudt, now Newhoudt-Druchen and a deaf Member of the South African Parliament, I was reminded of the early struggles we had had as a small group of deaf friends trying to initiate the project. We wanted to combat the segregation laws and the social and political oppression that deaf people faced at the time by setting up the multi-racial association. And here it was, still thriving, with a new sense of freedom for the deaf people, of whatever race, who gathered together there under the new democracy. I knew then our work had been right. We had been able to offer support during those long, painful times of oppression and sustain the hope that one day justice would come. The deaf staff showed us around and I was delighted by how much they had achieved. What a reward to know the pride they now took in their centre and to see how democracy had paved the way for deaf people to develop their potential and provide services for their own communities in the country.

How good it was to learn of the changes, for I had worked for many years with different cultures, languages and faiths, helping to build communities that are inclusive and give a sense of belonging, often where there have been rifts and divisions. How good it felt for me too, as I came home to Johannesburg, that the divisions within my own identity and faith were now healed. I grew up White in a Black country, Jewish among Catholics, deaf in a hearing world and my blindness at times separating me from my deaf community. Now I felt at peace.

What a homecoming it was. The reunion with my family was emotional. The Catholic priest welcomed into the bosom of his Jewish family with a Friday night Shabat celebration. What a wonderful opportunity for me to share with them all my Jewishness and for them to get to know me better as a deafblind man. I was no longer able to see to lipread my cousins as I had before but they took it in their stride, welcoming my communicator/guides, Lyn and Liz, to the family table. It was there that I picked up a napkin and put it on my head as a makeshift skullcap and began to recite the Kiddush, uniting the family in prayer. As Liz signed on to my hands to tell me that all around the table people had tears running down their cheeks, I knew I had finally come home.

My sixtieth birthday tea party was held a few days later on a hot, sunny afternoon in my cousin Dawn and her husband Steve's garden. I could smell the sweet fragrance of roses and sense the garden full of summer flowers just as I remembered it when I could see. There were many people there who knew me from all periods of my life, including my early childhood, and one by one they queued to talk to me. I communicated with some people through my communicator's skilful translation and others signed directly on to my hands. We had many hours of happy reminiscing.

There were people I had been at school with at St Vincent's School for the Deaf, and those Jewish children I had attended Hebrew class with, now grown with grandchildren of their own. There were people I had worked with at Greaterman's when I was a young accounts clerk and those with whom I studied for my priesthood at the seminary. I met Redemptorist confrères and someone I worked with as a volunteer at the cathedral when I was a young priest. There were deaf people from different denominations and creeds, to whom I had offered pastoral support and counselling when I worked in Johannesburg. There were friends from many places and, of course there was my family and my dear godfather, Robert. It was a very special occasion for all of us, as people shared memories and happy anecdotes of how we got to know each other.

My communicators worked tirelessly conveying to me not only conversations but emotions, facial expressions and descriptions of what people looked like with the passing years. They must have been exhausted! What was I doing with two women in tow, my Jewish cousins wanted to know. Were they nuns? If not, who were they? I chuckled and my family seemed relieved when they heard the full story of our friendship.

I met Lyn Atkinson in 1994 after travelling from Macau to England to give a lecture at the International Conference of Chaplains to the Deaf, in Canterbury. Pastoral workers from all denominations gathered there. Lyn and her husband Doug McLean were there running a stall for their specialist bookshop on deafness and deaf issues. After my lecture, I was told the news that there was severe disruption to the rail services due to a train strike. I would be unable to travel to my next destination, a conference on Usher Syndrome at Birmingham University. The anxious organisers, concerned about my poor sight, asked Lyn and Doug if they would drop me off in London to catch a train from there. They willingly agreed, providing I did not mind squeezing in with crates of books. When I arrived at the car with my case, I found that they were not, as everyone thought, going back to Gloucestershire, but heading for the very same conference in Birmingham.

It was a long journey but Lyn chatted away in sign throughout, keeping the signs small so they were within the narrow field of vision I still had then. We immediately became firm friends. I discovered that Lyn's two deaf daughters also had Usher syndrome. What I did not know until I met them again at the World Congress for the Deaf in Brisbane in 1999 was that Doug was also an established publisher. He offered to publish my life story should I ever write it, and I was able to tell him that I was already half way through. So there and then I had found myself a publisher and my book was beginning to become a reality.

Lyn introduced me to Liz Hansford, who works as an interpreter and also has a daughter with Usher syndrome. How good it is to be able to talk to the mothers of deaf young adults in sign language and to see their dedication in ensuring they will always be able to communicate no matter what the future brings. Liz instinctively knows how to tailor communication to my needs and so was my natural choice, together with Lyn, to travel with me for my journey to South Africa. We made an unlikely trio, these two agnostic, middle-aged women guiding a Catholic priest for his home-coming. No wonder my family were suspicious.

All too soon it was time to leave South Africa. When I left, my cousin Dawn gave me a bottle of Jewish wine, a box of *matzos* and other ingredients to take home for celebrating Passover. A couple of months later, back at Rainbow Court, I was introduced briefly to a Jewish deafblind man who had come to spend a few weeks there because his flat in London was being renovated. He was upset. It was almost Passover

219

and he would not be able to celebrate with his Jewish friends at the Jewish Deaf Club.

I knew how he must feel and when I got home I suddenly remembered the wine and the *matzos* that Dawn had given me. I went straight back to him and invited him to dinner for the first night of Passover. He was delighted - but what he did not know was that I was going to prepare a special Seder meal for him. I went back to my flat and felt in the fridge to see what suitable food I had. Fortunately, there were plenty of vegetables and some breast of chicken.

Then I had to draw on my memory of how my parents had celebrated Passover with me as a child, what order the Passover meal took, and how the meal was set out on the table by my mother. It all seemed such a long time ago. First I took out my old copy of the Haggadah, a book for Passover, although, being blind, I could not read it now. Next I prepared the table with my mother's white linen and silver cutlery, the silver goblet and two wine glasses. I knew that candles would be too hazardous for us but I placed two skullcaps and the Haggadah on the table and then the bitter herbs and cooked chicken and vegetables that I remembered so well. When everything was ready, with my cane I guided myself over to my friend's flat. He put his right arm on my right shoulder and together, two deafblind men, we made our way back to my flat - the deafblind leading the deafblind.

Then I escorted him to the table and took his right hand to touch the skullcap, the book, the silver goblet and the plate of *matzos*. He was stunned. He knew that I was a Catholic priest and here I was preparing a real Jewish meal.

Overwhelmed, he took my hand and placed it on each of his cheeks. I could feel his tears of joy. There was a great feeling of love between us as we stood together, the Jewish man and his friend, the Jewish converted Catholic priest.

We sat down and, in the traditional way, I began the Passover prayers making the blessings over the bitter herbs, wine and *matzos,* but this time using the deafblind manual alphabet on my friend's left hand. Finally, I served up the hot meal, which we ate in silence and darkness while our hearts were brightened with joy and happiness.

At the end of the meal I recited the song *Let us Build a New Jerusalem,* while we held our hands together, clapping them joyfully. He was delighted. Then, at the end of the evening, we walked in the darkness back along the path to his flat, I could tell that he had really enjoyed our Passover celebrations.both our hearts uplifted. At his front door he embraced me with a loving Jewish sign of peace - '*Shalom.*'

It was also a great moment of joy for me too because I had been able again to touch my own Jewish identity. The years of my childhood when I was brought up as a young Jewish boy remained very important to me. I felt the deepest appreciation of my parents for giving me my first understanding of religion. They were not educated people but had brought from Lithuania their deeply-held belief that their religion and culture were the most important things. These they shared with me as I grew, communicating without words in the best way they knew how. I owe the roots of my faith and spirituality to my parents and to my Jewish upbringing, and to the steady relationship with them and their families.

I have great gratitude to my parents for sending me, against their own wishes, as a boarder to a Catholic school for the deaf. Education was not the most important thing to them, but they could nevertheless see that for me it would be the gateway to my future. First and foremost the Catholic Sisters gave me communication. They gave me language - the means to interact with people - which has been so important to me since childhood. They gave me encouragement and the education I needed to express myself and to learn how to gain knowledge and information. They believed in me and saw my potential. Despite the pain and frustration I sometimes experienced as a deaf child, they taught me how to communicate with both deaf and hearing people, a skill that has been invaluable in my life and work. They helped me bridge the gap between my deaf community and the hearing world, and what I learned from the Sisters gave me the courage and determination to take up all the challenges I would face. They gave me the foundations from which I could learn other languages and this has helped me to break down barriers between people and cultures.

What my parents gave me, together with what the Sisters gave me, was the means of becoming whole and fulfilled. Without the spirituality, the communication and the education, my life as a deaf man would have been very different. These gave me what I needed to shape my life, to explore my religion and eventually to offer my service to God and to deaf and deafblind people through my Catholic priesthood.

The one thing that I struggled with during the process of my conversion to Christianity was the fear that I would lose the fundamental support of the closely-knit Jewish community that has always been a hallmark of that faith. In fact, it is more than simply a religion. Jewishness is a culture and a way of life and I wanted to preserve within myself the Jewish heritage first given to me by my parents. Although the door closed on me when I wished to become a rabbi, I now see the closing of that door as the opening of a new path to the Catholic faith.

In following this path I came to realise that while I did risk some human losses in terms of family and community, I also had much to gain. I could see Christianity expanding my horizons and opening doors to a spirituality and a new form of fellowship that was more inclusive than exclusive. To this day I see the roots of my faith in Judaism, but the stem and the branches are my adherence to the Gospel of Jesus Christ.

I always remember my mother's words: 'I do not understand your faith but I accept it so long as you do God's work with deaf people.' In doing this work I have always tried to reach beyond barriers of faith. The reconciliation with my family after my mother's death was very important to me. So was the Mass of thanksgiving that I gave at the Holy Redeemer College in Washington DC after receiving my doctorate. It was a truly multicultural celebration. Thirty friends with different faiths and from different parts of the world were there. There were readings from the New Testament by Catholics and from the Old Testament by my Jewish cousin Dawn.

Over the years, I have been asked the same question over and over again. 'Why did you, as a Jew, become a Catholic?' I would answer 'Because this was what God chose for me in order that I could give my life to deaf and deafblind people of all faiths.' God blessed me not only with faith but with an education that I could draw upon.

T. S. Eliot wrote in his poem *The Rock* that the wisdom, knowledge and information of the twentieth century have taken us further away from God:

Where is the Life we have lost in the living?
Where is the wisdom we have lost in knowledge?
Where is the knowledge we have lost in information?

For me it is the reverse. Learning, information and knowledge are gifts from God that have enriched my life and brought me closer to Him. Without them I would have had a very different life experience and some very different journeys. I would not have understood God's calling or become a priest or been able to undertake my lifelong service in His name.

In this book, I have written of only some of those journeys, but all of them have had their joys and their sorrows. Out of those joys and sorrows have always come new beginnings, new mystery and new enrichment as I follow my destiny as a human being.

224

Illustrations

1. My maternal grandfather, Abraham Goodman.

2. My maternal grandmother, Shifre Goldberg.

3. My maternal grandparents' shop in Lithuania.

4. My mother, Yetta Goodman.

5. My father, Abe Axelrod, at work in Johannesburg.

6. My mother and father on their honeymoon in Durban, 1937.

7. Aged one with our dog Lucky, 1943.

8. Aged two with my mother. I was still unable to walk.

9. Aged three, just after the diagnosis of my profound deafness.

10. Aunt May and Uncle Oscar, my mother's brother and sister.

11. Aged seven with my mother and father.

12. The Rosary.

13. Jewish deaf children with our Hebrew teacher, Ralph Hahn. I am the second from the right in the front row, sucking a sweet.

14. Aged thirteen with my father after my Bar Mitzvah.

15. A concert at the Jewish Deaf Hostel to celebrate the Jewish Festival of Purim. I am wearing the crown. Johannesburg, 1954.

16. Celebrating Chanukah at the Jewish Deaf Hostel. I am fifteen and the tallest.

17. First year students at St John Vianney Seminary, Pretoria, 1967. I am kneeling.

18. The congregation at my Ordination to the Priesthood in the Cathedral of Christ the King, Johannesburg. 28 November 1970.

225

19. Deaf pupils of St Vincent's School for the Deaf and Sisters at my Ordination to the Priesthood.

20. My mother leading me to be ordained.

21. My Ordination by the Right Reverend Ernest A. Green, then Bishop of Port Elizabeth.

22. Giving my first blessing at the Ordination – the Jewish blessing to my mother.

23. At the end of my Ordination with Bishop Green.

24. Giving Holy Communion.

25. My first Mass as an ordained priest, at the Church of the Immaculate Conception in my home parish of Rosebank, Johannesburg. 29 November 1970.

26. With my mother and Bishop Green the day after my Ordination.

27. The photograph of me as a newly ordained priest that hung on my mother's wall.

28. Old pupils at St Vincent's School for the Deaf after my Ordination, 1970.

29. Staff from St Thomas' School for the Deaf, near King William's Town, Eastern Cape Province, visiting St Vincent's School for the Deaf, Johannesburg, after my Ordination. 1970.

30. Giving Holy Communion to deaf children in Cape Town, 1971.

31. My mother's grave in Johannesburg Jewish Cemetery, 1974.

32. At The Western Wall, Jerusalem, 1978. I am second from the right.

33. My skullcaps, prayer shawl and phylacteries.

34. Singapore. An evening celebration, 1985.

35. A farewell from the Singapore deaf people at the airport, 1985.

36. With deaf children at the Speech and Language Centre, Macau, 1991.

37. Tea Ceremony at a wedding in Hong Kong, 1992.

38. Talking to a group of deaf pupils at St Augustine School for the Deaf, near Manila, Philippines, 1995.

39. In the People's Republic of China, at The Great Wall, with Simon Chan Wai Hung, Alice Lao Iok Ieng and Noven Li Yuk Lin. 1999.

40. At work with the Board of the Macau Deaf Association.

41. Demonstrating to the Governor of Macau the computers donated by the Lions' Club. 1999.

42. With the Governor of Macau for the unveiling of the plaque to mark the official opening of the new Social Services Centre for Deaf People in Macau, August 1999.

43. Farewell from the deaf people of Macau and Hong Kong. Hong Kong, 1999.

44. Two deaf delegates, Lindsay Sunne from South Africa and John Chan representing China, place the doctoral hood over my shoulders. Gallaudet University, Washington DC, USA, 2001.

45. Receiving my Honorary Doctorate from I. King Jordan, President of the University.

46. President I. King Jordan signs on my hands. Behind us the ceremony is projected onto a large screen so that the deaf audience can see the signing.

47. With Steven Walker, staff interpreter for deafblind people, and Dr. Donalda K. Ammons, Professor of Foreign Languages at Gallaudet University.

48. Blessing the Turf for a new building at Deafblind UK. Peterborough, UK. 2001

49. A newspaper cutting from the Peterborough Evening Telegraph, 2003.

50. A conversation with Sister Chris CFS, at St John the Evangelist Church, Islington, London, 2004.

51. Mass for the Brentwood Deaf Community at St Mary and St Ethelburga Church, Barking, London, 2004.

52. A conversation with HRH The Princess Royal at the Sense Awards. London, 2004.

53. A return visit to the Deaf Community of Cape Town, September 2004. Stephen Lombard and I are in front of the plaque to commemorate the opening in 1994.

54. A Communion service at the Deaf Community of Cape Town during the same visit. 2004.

55. A Communion service at the Deaf Community of Cape Town during the same visit. 2004.

56. With Bishop Bernard Longley. Mass at Westminster Cathedral, London, to celebrate the launch of my Ministry to Deafblind People. November 2004.

57. With Bishop Bernard, incensing the altar at the Mass, Westminster Cathedral, London. 27 November 2004.

58. At St John the Evangelist Church, Islington, London, wearing my Redemptorist habit, black with a white collar. 2004.